# CODEPENDENCY & MEN

## Where Early Attachment, Gender Role, and Adrenal Fatigue Meet

**Mary Crocker Cook,** D.Min, LMFT, LAADC, CADCII
Author of *Awakening Hope* and *Afraid to Let Go*

**Edited by Howard Scott Warshaw, MA, ME, LMFT**

## Codependency & Men

ISBN: 978-1-61170-147-0

Email: marycook@connectionscounselingassociates.com

Printed in the USA and UK on acid-free paper.

 Robertson Publishing™
www.RobertsonPublishing.com

To purchase additional copies of this book go to:
    amazon.com
    barnesandnoble.com
    www.rp–author.com/mcook

# Dedication

*For my father, William G. Crocker*

*I miss you*

# Table of Contents

At its heart, Codependency is a set of behaviors developed to manage the anxiety that comes when our primary attachments are formed with people who are inconsistent or unavailable in their response to us. Our anxiety-based responses to life can include over-reactivity, image management, unrealistic beliefs about our limits, and attempts to control the reality of others to the point where we lose our boundaries, self-esteem, and even our own reality. Ultimately, Codependency is a chronic stress disease, which can devastate our immune system and lead to systemic and even life-threatening illness. — *Mary Crocker Cook*

# MAN TIPS

## A GUIDE TO BEING A REAL MAN

*Man Hugs*

*The do's and don'ts*

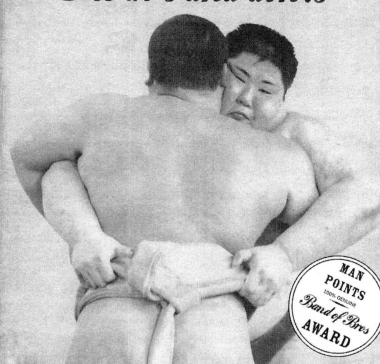

MAN
POINTS
100% GENUINE
*Band of Bros*
AWARD

# THE MECHANICS OF A MAN HUG

YOU WILL NEED:

A WILLING MAN

1. BEGIN WITH A TRADITIONAL FIRM HANDSHAKE

2. KEEPING YOUR HAND CLASPED WITH YOUR BUDDY, WRAP YOUR LEFT ARM AROUND THEIR SHOULDER

3. SLAP YOUR FRIEND'S BACK THREE TIMES. THE BACK SLAP IS KEY

4. RELEASE EMBRACE

WARNING:

MAN HUGGING IS NOT APPROPRIATE WITH EVERY MAN YOU COME IN CONTACT WITH. IT CARRIES WITH IT A KIND OF INTIMACY THAT SHOULD BE RESERVED FOR CLOSE FRIENDS AND FAMILY.

DON'T TRY A MAN HUG WITH A NEW ACQUAINTANCE.

DON'T EVER MAN HUG WHEN NOT FULLY CLOTHED, UNLESS OF COURSE YOU'RE A SUMO WRESTLER.

IT IS ESSENTIAL THAT YOU NEVER MAN HUG WITHOUT THE BACK SLAP. THIS MAKES IT MORE MANLY AND LESS CUDDLY.

## CHAPTER ONE

## *Is this book for me? Codependency defined as an attachment disruption issue*

I chose to write about Codependency and men because I have always wondered why I had more self-identified codependent women than men in my practice. Do men just have better boundaries? Are they less anxious? Two decades of practice as an LMFT tells me differently. Here's an example:

*Kevin is a 37 year old mid-level software manager and father of two small children. Kevin's wife is a "stay-at-home Mom." He is seeking counseling because he is tired of her complaints about his angry outbursts. Kevin is shocked himself! He feels deeply ashamed after raising his voice to his wife or children during these occasional eruptions. This is precisely not the man he would like to be.*

*A brief history reveals that Kevin has long standing resentment towards his wife due to her emotional volatility, which she describes as being "passionate." His father modeled passivity in the face of Kevin's mother's emotional unpredictability, and Kevin does his best to emulate his father's apparent "calm." The unspoken agreement in Kevin's marriage is that he is to be the "grounding force" that allows his wife to be as emotionally unstable as she needs and wants to be. So when Kevin becomes angry the entire family seems to de-stabilize and he feels tremendous shame and guilt – like he has failed. When he thinks about it further, he suspects maybe his father's wine intake had something to do with his ability to "check-out" when Kevin's mom was "off the hook." He is hoping counseling will provide him with more tools to "hold it together better" and have more self-control without drinking like his father did.*

In a typical counseling setting Kevin might be seen as depressed, or referred to couple's counseling to improve communication. He might even be referred to a man's group for support to increase his personal boundaries and sense of self. I doubt anyone would have said he is "Codependent." As you read through the text you will discover why I would quickly identify Kevin as codependent.

If I am completely honest, I'm also attempting to understand my father. He came from a childhood devoid of nurturing and financial security, yet replete with emotional and physical abuse. Consequently he entered marriage and parenting with few intimacy tools. He mellowed with age, enough for me to attempt personal conversations with him, but he still seemed puzzled by the idea of an internal world and claimed he had never had dreams, just ambition. He did what was in front of him as perfectly as possible. What he really had was the male persona of a hard working farm child, honed to a fine edge as a career Naval officer.

When I imagine my father in counseling (which is a stretch) he would most likely have been confused by my distrust of his attachment to me. He would have felt he demonstrated his trustworthiness by providing for my needs and education. Since he wasn't introspective he couldn't see the value I held for his internal world. I went through a period in high school (after his latest year-long deployment) when I refused to call him "Dad" and only re-ferred to him by rank. I was telling him I didn't like the fact his clear priority was work, not family. He never asked me about it though, just waited me out. Eventually I shifted back to "Dad."

When I consider the men (like my father) I have treated in psychotherapy, I recognize the challenge I face as a counselor. These men are in counseling due to an insistent wife, troubled child or their own addiction. They suffer a lack of connection with the people they say they love most. Chronically accused of being over controlling or emotionally absent, they feel at sea when their wives and children claim to be lonely in their presence. How can these people feel "unloved" when (from his perspective) he has dedicated his life to their welfare?

Some of these men will express their lack of vitality and emotional engage-ment though endless service. They are hyperaware of the moods, needs and preferences of loved ones, yet their self-neglect can be profound. This text examines how a lack of secure early attachment with caregivers can re-sult in the tendency to self-abandon while managing connections with sig-nificant others. Their anxiety and distrust of the connection of others will manifest in anxious monitoring, over-giving, passive aggressive approaches to anger and chronic worry. For them, failure to anticipate and meet the needs of others equals abandonment.

**Codependency Defined**

One of the greatest challenges when addressing Codependency, male or female, is the lack of unified agreement on its definition. In my text, Awakening Hope, I proposed the following definition of Codependency:

*At its heart, Codependency is a set of behaviors developed to manage the anxiety that comes when our primary attachments are formed with people who are inconsistent or unavailable in their response to us. Our anxiety-based responses to life can include over-reactivity, image management, unrealistic beliefs about our limits, and attempts to control the reality of others to the point where we lose our boundaries, self-esteem and even our own reality. Ultimately, Codependency is a chronic stress disease, which can devastate our immune system and lead to systemic and even life-threatening illness.* [1]

My entire definition for codependency is based on codependency as a result of early attachment interruptions. Early unavailable or unpredictable caretaker response can lead to several dysfunctional relationship tendencies.

Briefly, early theorists like John Bowlby and Margaret Main conducted several key experiments to determine the effects of parent availability (or lack thereof) on a child's ability to form attachments with others throughout the course of their life. This research noted the emergence of three basic "attachment" styles:

**Secure**: Relationships provide a safe and reliable "home base." Able to feel connected even when separated, trusting the mutual connection in the relationship.

**Anxious**: Always vigilant for the relationship attachment to be broken, anxious and fearful of being abandoned or driving the other person to leave. This often leads to vigilant, intrusive behaviors with poor boundaries and self-definition.

**Avoidant**: Also anxious and fearful about abandonment. Cannot rely on close attachments, always has a "Plan B" for when the relationship ends. This person tends to be fiercely independent, with walls instead of boundaries.

**NOTE: To learn more about your own intimacy style, I encourage you to take the Intimacy Inventory provided in Appendix A.**

I cover the research on Attachment Theory and adult attachment behaviors more extensively in my first book, *Awakening Hope. A Developmental, Behavioral, Biological Approach to Codependent Treatment (2011).*

However, it is important to note that **attachment experts are unanimous in their conclusion that there are no gender differences in secure infant attachment. In their analysis of the research literature pertaining to gender difference in infant attachment, Feeney and Noller's research demonstrates clearly that men and women are equally likely to develop any of the three attachment styles.** [2]

This means that males are just as likely to develop attachment-based codependency as women, yet they do not get identified as frequently. This led me to consider the significance gender role plays in the identification and treatment, because gender role is the most obvious differentiating factor

Let's experiment with this thought

*Joe is a 34 year old software engineer, and has been married to Susan for 5 years. They have a young daughter, Ashley, who is 3 years old. Joe is the oldest of 3 children, with a younger sister and brother. His father was a pilot who flew internationally and was frequently away from home. His mother operated as a single parent. She had been raised to "look good" no matter what the circumstances, so if she struggled she would never let her children know. Joe, being the oldest, was frequently her confidante and he was well aware she'd started seeing her doctor more regularly for help with her sleep. She had multiple pill bottles by her bedside, and there were many times when he would get everyone ready for school because he was unable to fully rouse his mother. She would still be groggy driving them to school which was scary. Consequently, as soon as they were able to ride their bikes to school, the children chose to do so.*

*Susan is troubled by Joe's mother's pill use, which has increased. Susan refuses to let Joe's mother babysit Ashley unsupervised. Joe completely concurs. Joe's father is often competitive with Joe financially, and his conversation is peppered with "one-upmanship" comments that Joe tends to brush off as "just Dad," and lets his Dad be the "big guy" knowing that his stock package is lucrative. He has never mentioned his concern about his mother's pill use to either parent – he just fills in the gaps to make sure his mother is never alone with Ashley.*

*Joe "fills in the gaps" in a lot of ways. When he notices that Susan has forgotten detergent at the store he quietly picks it up the next time he's out. When Susan appears tired he drops his laptop and takes over Ashley's bathtime and reading schedule for the rest of the night. Joe is also a better cook than Susan, so he begins meal preparation when he arrives home earlier. He is willing to listen and give feedback to Susan when she worries about Ashley or her own family.*

*If Joe were honest with himself, he'd admit that he monitors Susan for signs that she may be developing a substance abuse or mental health problem like his Mother. He is terrified of re-creating his parents' marriage.*

For Joe, vigilance is mandatory. He identifies himself as the solution to all problems (real or perceived) and expects himself to have the energy and competence to handle them. Keeping everything smooth is vital to his sense of personal well-being, and no sacrifice of self is too great to make this happen. Dropping the ball and rocking the boat would equal relationship rupture.

Other men will express their lack of vitality and emotional connection through exaggerating their male gender role. They will over focus on providing, achievement, overt control, criticism, intrusive problem solving and emotional disengagement. They may use alcohol and drugs to manage the stress of constant performance. They see their connections to others hanging in the balance. Failure to produce will equal abandonment.

Now let's tell Joe's story a bit differently

*Joe is a 34 year old software engineer, and has been married to Susan for 5 years. They have a young daughter, Ashley, who is 3 years old. Joe is the* oldest of 3 children, with a younger sister and brother. His father was a pilot who flew internationally and was frequently away from home. His mother operated as a single parent. She had been raised to "look good" no matter what the circumstances, so if she struggled she would never let her children know. Joe, being the oldest, was frequently her confidante and he was well aware she'd started seeing her doctor more regularly for help with her sleep. She had multiple pill bottles by her bedside, and there were many times when he would get everyone ready for school because he was unable to fully rouse his mother. She would still be groggy driving them to school which was scary. Consequently, as soon as they were able to ride their bikes to school, the children chose to do so.

Susan is troubled by Joe's mother's pill use, which has increased. Susan refuses to let Joe's mother babysit Ashley unsupervised. Joe thinks Susan is over-reacting, and points out that his Dad is usually there anyway. The last thing he is willing to do is upset his mother – which will piss off his Dad and create a situation Joe will have to manage. Joe's father is often competitive with Joe financially, and his conversation is peppered with "one-upmanship" comments Joe finds amusing given his own financially lucrative stock package. He goes along with his Dad's behavior, though Susan notices that Joe drinks more when he is with his father.

Joe is a high achiever, and personally demanding because he works hard, provides for the family, and spends way more time with Ashley than his Dad spent with him. He picks her up from day care three times a week, and barbecues on the weekend to make things easier for Susan, he also happens to be a better cook. When Joe notices that Susan has forgotten detergent at the store, he gets irritated because her only job is to take care of the house and Ashley, and he can't imagine what she must be doing with her time. Even if he doesn't say something he still feels resentful when he has to do chores on top of his regular routine.

When Susan appears tired he finds this a little confusing. He begins to support her by suggesting more efficient time-management strategies, and he puts down his laptop and takes over Ashley's bath-time and reading schedule for the rest of the night. Joe is willing to listen and give feedback to Susan when she worries about Ashley or her own family, but he gets frustrated when she doesn't seem to implement his feedback.

*If Joe were honest with himself, he'd admit that he provides and problem solves for Susan to prevent development of a substance abuse or mental health problem like his Mother. He is terrified of re-creating his parents' marriage*

**Now, I would like you take just a minute and jot down in the margins what you were thinking about Joe during each version of his story. Did you relate to one more than the other?**

Many of the men I've treated (in over twenty years in the business) can identify with one of these versions of Joe. I have counseled men individual-ly, led groups in all-male residential addiction treatment settings and have trained several thousand students as counselors for the last two decades. In these roles, men have entrusted me with their fears about aging, worries about their legacies, distrust of their own parenting and relationships skills, conflicts with co-workers and loved ones and feeling lost. They have shared their burdens and their aloneness, often haunted by the feeling they should be doing more... should be more. They have shared their worries that bald-ing means they will have to settle for a lesser partner and their inadequacy because their bank account is not as large as their heart.

It is for these men (and their big hearts) that I write this book. I write with sincere hope that these men will learn to be happier and healthier. That they can learn to spend less time with me and more time in intimate loving relationships.

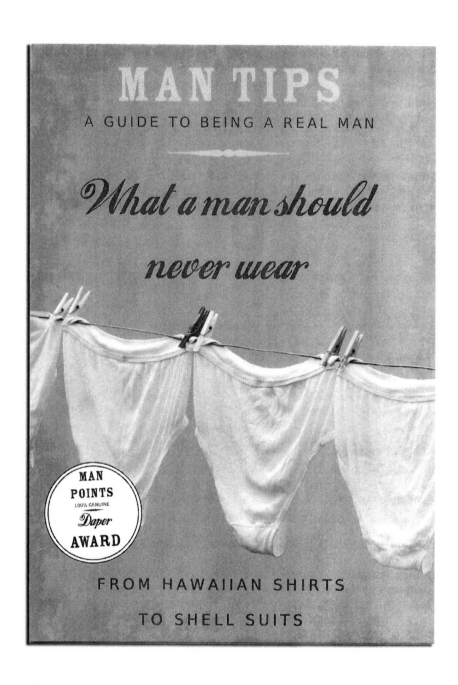

There are some things that men cannot and should not wear.

Be advised to follow this guide.

**BEADED NECKLACES.** This makes you look like you are hanging out on the beach circa 1990's.

**HAWAIIAN SHIRTS.** Whoa there. These are a little garish and crazy.

**HOOPED EARRINGS.** Are you a pirate? I don't think so!

**BUM BAGS.** Very 1990's Dad . . . should not be worn.

**TRACK SUITS.** The days of matching shell suits are long gone. . . leave them in the past.

**FIGURE HUGGING SWIM TRUNKS (AKA BANANA HAMMOCKS).** Unless you're a professional swimmer don't do it. It makes everyone uncomfortable.

**MEDALLIONS.** "A-Team." Need we say more?

**LEATHER TROUSERS.** Whilst they were once so "sexy it hurts," today . . . not so much. Only rock starts can get away with wearing these.

**Y-FRONTS.** Emm. . . do we need to explain this?

**BASEBALL CAP BACK TO FRONT.** So 1980's teenage boy look. This is not for a man!

**SOCKS AND SANDALS.** The biggest fashion faux pas there is!

**CAMOUFLAGE.** Unless you are in the army this is just not necessary.

**COMEDY PANTS, SOCKS AND TIES.** It is far better to tell a joke than to be a joke!

CHAPTER TWO

## *Male Gender Role and Gender Role Strain*

### What Do We Know About Male Gender Role?

*Fred is a 32 year old male, seeking help due to the recent break-up of his relationship with Tina, a woman who abuses prescription medications. Initially he wondered how he could help Tina "see" that her drug abuse and emotional instability were causing problems in their relationship.*

*Historically, Fred was an only child raised by a highly explosive, erratic father and a placating, dissociative mother. Communication was unidirectional from father to son, and continually critical. He actively remembers "disappearing" around the age of ten by making a conscious effort to stay under the radar. He never brought attention to himself by asking for anything and focused exclusively on intellectual development. Now he heads a biomedical research laboratory.*

*All of Fred's relationships have been chaotic so he adopts the role of "audience" and advice giver. With Tina, he attempts to bring order to her chaotic and emotionally labile world. He describes himself as highly adaptive, with no awareness or interest in his own internal world. However, he believes he is highly attuned to Tina's thoughts and feelings.*

*Fred meets with a local chemical dependency counselor in an attempt to figure out Tina's motivations and thoughts (even though she is not in the room). The counselor asks Fred about his feelings and thoughts in responses to current email exchanges and conversations with Tina. This puzzles and annoys Fred who does not see the relevance of his own internal world. He finds questions about his feelings a "waste of time" since he is there to find a way to help Tina. Fred knows it's up to him to solve the problem but he has no awareness of how he may be contributing to the problem.*

*When we read about Fred, his over-focus on Tina is obvious. However, it is easy to dismiss this behavior or take it for granted. Fred's approach to assisting Tina is a familiar male-gender-based response. Logical problem solving is something he learned to do growing up in a culture which has a lot to say about how men should act as "real" men.*

### Gender Role defined

Gender role is generally defined as a set of attitudes, behaviors, and self-presentation methods ascribed to members of a certain biological sex. This includes norms for behavior, which some researchers have started to call "the rules of masculinity" or "masculine ideology."

Some researchers have also tried to explore whether there is a "universal masculine" gender role that can be seen in all cultures during all times. This proves to be quite difficult, but some social roles have been highlighted. [3]

Specifically, those are:
1. Provider: Secure and provide resources
2. Protector: Defend others and territory

In general, I have noticed that many Codependent men have adopted a "self" based on either an exaggerated male gender role or a reaction to a gender role conflict. The challenge when working with male codependents is to address their gender role exaggeration or conflict directly to see how this gender role "self" has been created as a result of early attachment disruption.

Few men realize how much of their lives are lived in pursuit of the values our culture has traditionally associated with masculinity. These values – a primary focus on work, logical thinking and always being in emotional control – have many benefits to men and their families. When taken to extremes, the pursuit of traditional masculine values becomes a cage for feelings, a stranglehold on life itself. [4]

Many researchers examine larger cultural trends of male gender roles, however Levant, [5-6] a major player in this field, refined traditional American masculinity into seven principles:

Levant's Seven Principles of American Masculinity

1. Restrict emotions
2. Avoid being feminine
3. Focus on toughness and aggression
4. Be self-reliant
5. Make achievement the top priority
6. Be non-relational about sexuality
7. Be homophobic

It is important to note that, although these principles are a general trajectory for many men, the particular manifestation/expression may vary significantly depending on individual and sub-cultural differences.

**NOTE: I have provided a questionnaire in Appendix B based on Levant's seven principles of male gender role. When you have your scores, continue reading to see what the subscales mean.**

Let's examine each of them in greater detail...

## 1) Restrict emotions

According to John Donovan,[7] a 25 year veteran of ManAlive men's groups in Sacramento, most men are profoundly detached from their bodies. They often do not register pain, fatigue, temperature or illness.

Hough and Hardy note how sports can train boys to neglect their bodies. "Sports and playground peer groups are key indoctrination agents. The so called 'male' value of not showing pain, discomfort, or physical vulnerability is communicated clearly and often. When a typical boy is hurt, he winces but clears his face before he turns back to his peers. Whatever feelings of pain that do show through are automatically denied, 'It's nothing.' Later, with practice, that denial will become unconscious as he successfully anesthetizes his body against all pain." [8]

This dissociation from the body extends to emotional disengagement. Without access to his feelings a man can't help but lose track of who he is, what his priorities are and what is normal for him.

This ideal that men live up to in public is usually expressed in negative form: Don't wear your feelings on your sleeve (men are not supposed to let their deeper feelings show). Don't be too emotionally visible to others (it's safer to be emotionally opaque than obvious). After years of practicing deceptions like this, men wind up emotionally confused and out of touch. [9]

## 2) Avoid being feminine

David & Brannon [10] describe "no sissy stuff" (distance from femininity) as being one of the four standards of American masculinity. The disidenitification from the female described in the therapeutic literature is a bedrock requirement for men in their process of gender identification.

*Effeminate* is a term frequently applied to womanly behavior, demeanor, style and appearance displayed by a male. This term typically connotes criticism or ridicule of these behaviors (as opposed to merely describing a male as feminine, which could be non-judgmental). The term *effeminate* is most often used by people who subscribe to the widespread view that males should display traditional masculine traits and behaviors.

The definition of what constitutes effeminate behavior varies greatly depending on the social and cultural context as well as the time period. While some effeminate behaviors evoke stereotypical impressions of homosexuality in some people, others may simply view the behavior as unmanly without questioning the sexual orientation of the person in question.

## 3) Focus on toughness and aggression

Donovan has learned over time that the "angry man" image, a man who has a hair-trigger angry response, is usually a myth. The ManAlive program teaches how the "angry man" is more often a response to experiencing a threat to their "image," which triggers a fight or flight response. When the sympathetic nervous system gets triggered – breathing is more rapid, heart rate increases, blood pressure goes up – men call this stimulated response "anger." In fact, anger is more often a response to injustice. What these men are experiencing is not anger but an arousal state. This is key information for men to have because, as they learn to interrupt this hyperarousal, they have more opportunity to connect with what they may actually be feeling.

One of the more disturbing aspects of male behavior I've observed working in male treatment centers is the way they use humor, which is often aggressive, dismissive, diminishing, hurtful and demeaning. I remember telling some male colleagues once after listening to their "banter" for about 30 minutes that I would be in tears if people spoke to me this way. Donovan pointed out that this often comes from competitiveness which pervades many male encounters. This style of communication definitely discourages intimacy of any kind.

Dissociation from the body and emotions – numbness – is a basic requirement of the male ideal. Hardy and Hough point out that the patriarchal culture's influence is so strong on this point that it interferes with men ever recognizing that pain is a normal indicator of a problem. And as the pain or discomfort increases, men are forced to choose between two problematic alternatives:

*If I admit I'm sick then I must do something about it. That may entail seeing a doctor which implies I'm weak, not in control of myself, not tough enough.*

*However, if I don't get help, I'll get sicker and more vulnerable, really helpless.* [11]

Men demonstrate this ambivalence through forgetfulness, procrastination and even by manipulating others to "insist" they go for help (thus relieving them of having to "own" their potential neediness or vulnerability).

## 4) Be self-reliant

The majority of research I've reviewed describes an intense male value on independence and what appears to be an almost phobic response to dependence. In fact, for many men it's not even an option to ask for assistance or to admit they "don't know." This places tremendous pressure on men to deny their vulnerability and need for information which makes detachment from relationships easier.

*Men often confuse emotional control with personal independence.* They tend to believe containment of feelings is the truest measure of real independence. [11]

Men are generally reluctant to compromise their independence for the sake of connection with others. They equate independence with being alone, separate, and uncommunicative.

It also strikes me that male-to-male bonding can create a gender role conflict, as it challenges the myth of full independence. Heroism is an exception. In fact, heroism has a long tradition as part of manhood. Bonds formed through natural disaster or war are exceptions to the typical "self-reliance" rules. These are opportunities for men to experience a type of connection with each other that is ordinarily prohibited by the "rules" of manhood.

### 5) Make achievement the top priority

Donovan described the seemingly instinctive ability of men to determine the power structure in any relationship (and their place within that power structure). It can be as primitive as "reading" a room to determine "whose ass I may have to kick" and begin preparing for this possibility. Competition is the norm and there can be only one "Alpha." Women have a correlate, which is to survey a room to establish the most attractive woman and her own place in the beauty hierarchy.

The masculine ideal of perfection creates a hyper-sensitivity to any nuance of imperfection. Any man who commits his life to the perfectionistic ideal of masculinity is going to feel like a failure. The people around him will feel abused and oppressed by him. The only way to do things is his way, the right way, the ideal way. Every man who succeeds at this game will wind up in the same place: Alone in his victory. At the top of the pyramid there's no room for anyone else. [12]

If you are locked in this ideal you are locked into a belief system that says you are nothing until you prove it – you are either on the top and okay or on the bottom and worth nothing.

### 6) Be non-relational about sexuality

Objectifying sex is connected to the fear of acknowledging the relational aspect of sexuality – the intimacy needs that "merging" through sexuality can create. The experience of intimacy can lead a man to vulnerability. It can threaten his "image" of being completely self-reliant and independent.

It may also open him to awareness of his desire for intimacy. There is a strong connection between power and virility. Evidencing virility by obtaining younger partners (trophy wives) announces a man's overall viability and competitive value. Men in the media are rarely portrayed as reluctant to have sex. They are ready at any-moment, indiscriminant about their partners and the emphasis is clearly on his performance – much like any athletic endeavor. When we see People magazine's "Sexiest Man of the Year" issue sitting next to Men's Health magazine's "Let's Get Ripped" issue, it's clear they are not exploring a man's sensitivity and emotional development! Just like in the work arena the message is: "You ARE your performance."

Many feminist writers have pointed out that objectifying sex is very much a part of the American culture. We use sexuality to sell products, media events and magazines. Our notions about sexuality are often distorted by these images. Women as well as men often have unrealistic expectations about sexuality – especially our own. Surrounded by air-brushed images, it is painful to inhabit our own bodies at times due to the feelings of failure and inability to "measure up" to these images.

## 7) Be homophobic

Finally, Donovan points out that the perception of homosexual relationships is that someone will need to be "the woman," triggering an intense fear of being "feminine" or reduced to "female" which does not have the cultural status of "male." This was eye-opening to me as a woman. I remember a time when I was younger when I felt "cheated" in some ways by being female – perceiving men as having far more options in the world. This memory helps me relate to men's homophobic fears in a very personal way.

In most cultures, effeminacy is traditionally considered a weakness, if not a vice, indicative of other negative character traits and often involving a negative insinuation of homosexual tendencies or sexual passivity.

Examples of behavior noncompliant with conventional masculinity have included:

- Interest in women's fashion.
- Effusive emotional expressions among other males.

- Cross-dressing or use of makeup.
- Adoption of stereotypically feminine mannerisms.

## Gender Role Conflict and Strain

What if a man does not identify with Levant's Principles? In fact, many men find them repulsive and wind up distancing themselves from stereotypical male imaging, which can result in what is referred to as a gender role conflict

### GENDER ROLE CONFLICT

Any discussion of male codependency, even one rooted in early attachment disruption, must address the pressures of the social-norm context for male development. These pressures are often referred to in the literature as "gender role strain." Gender role strain in men has been identified as either the failure to fulfill male role expectations or the traumatic fulfillment of these expectations, and their negative consequences. One proposed cause of gender role strain is the early gender role socialization process which begins within the family context and is supported by a larger cultural socialization based on patriarchy.

There are specific patterns of negative consequences that emerge for men during their experience with gender role strain. These patterns are well researched and referred to as "gender role conflict." For example, many men restrict their emotions. This may have positive consequences such as the ability to stay cool in a crisis situation, but a disadvantage would be the inability to emotionally connect in a relationship. The man may experience gender role strain if he does express feelings in the relationship, and concerns about the loneliness and detachment that could follow this choice would be gender role conflict.

Hardy and Hough state that men "are trying to live up to an ideal of how they, as men, should feel and act. And most likely, many of these men harbor deep within themselves a notion that they are failing in life." [13] O'Neil [14] breaks down different types of gender role conflict as well as defining devaluations, restrictions and violations thusly:

"Gender role devaluations are negative critiques of self or others when conforming to, deviating from, or violating stereotypic gender role norms of ideal masculinity. Devaluations result in lessening of personal status, stature, or positive regard." [15]

This devaluation can happen in four different ways:

### 1) Gender Role Conflict within the man

Private *experience* of negative emotions and thoughts labeled as gender role devaluations, restrictions, and violations.

*Dan has been having an increasingly hard time sleeping. He worries about the way he is perceived at work. Dan acknowledges he has always struggled with perfectionism which led to procrastination in high school and college. His friends would tease him about "pulling the trigger" as he would debate and ruminate over papers and presentations. He is worried at this point that his procrastination pattern makes him look weak in front of his boss. He finds himself dreading work, convinced that today could be the day when his "weakness" and failure to "man up" on his project could become visible in front of the entire department.*

### 2) Gender Role Conflict expressed toward others

Men's expressed gender role problems that potentially devalue, restrict, or violate someone else.

"Gender role restrictions occur when confining others or oneself to stereotypic norms of masculinity ideology. Restrictions result in controlling people's behavior, limiting one's personal potential, and decreasing human freedom."

*Gary takes enormous pride in his role as departmental lead at a local software company. A fan of war movies and war-based video games, Gary loves competition in any form, and is quick to evaluate department politics in terms of "for us" or "against us." He is highly protective of his team and believes they value this about him. Lately Gary has become frustrated with his supervisor, perceiving him to be unwilling to serve as the political "firewall" Gary believes is necessary for the team to grow. Gary is finding it increasingly hard to be civil in departmental meetings, barely concealing his contempt for his supervisor as he thinks "For God's sake, grow a pair."*

### 3) Gender Role Conflict experienced from others

Men's interpersonal experience of gender role conflict from people with whom they interact can result in feeling personally devalued, restricted, or violated.

"Gender role violations result from harming oneself, harming others or being harmed by others when deviating from or conforming to gender role norms of masculinity ideology. To be violated is to be victimized and abused, causing psychological and physical pain."[15]

*Joe has always loved the ocean and particularly loves to sail. After working an extra job for several years, he has finally been able to purchase his own sailboat and is thrilled to join a local yacht club. Initially, Joe thoroughly enjoys meeting the other members, hoping that with the ocean in common he will develop a strong group of friends. As he becomes more involved, he begins to feel somewhat uneasy at the Wednesday evening business meetings. The meetings are often contentious, especially after several rounds of drinks and Joe finds himself withdrawing from the aggressive, hostile banter among the men. The other men recognize Joe's discomfort and begin to second guess his membership, coming to believe he really isn't "one of us" after all. Joe is discouraged as he concludes they are right, and withdraws his membership.*

### 4) Gender Role Conflict experienced from role transitions

Gender role transitions are events in a man's gender role development that alter or challenge his gender role self-assumptions and consequently produce positive life changes.

*David has managed a successful string of restaurants for years, and enjoyed a reputation among his managers for being hard to understand but fair. He has taken comfort in his independence as a business owner, resisting authority even as child. As a child of an absent, alcoholic father he had learned to problem solve independently early, relying on and trusting his own judgment. David has recently been diagnosed with a degenerative bone disease and finds himself fighting fatigue for the first time in his life.*

*Initially, David does not include his wife as he takes his medical tests and searches for a diagnosis. However, his increasing silence and withdrawal has begun to create a martial problem, and his wife suspects he is having an affair. In fact, his wife has asked for marriage counseling because she feels even lonelier in the marriage than she has over the years.*

*As David looks at her tear-stained face he realizes that he must either include his wife into his medical condition and treatment plans or he will wind up alone as his own father had. After several nights of disturbed sleep, he finally wakes up and realizes that the only way to change his family pattern is to challenge his own fear of being "needy." He loves her and decides he is not willing to lose her to keep his pride.*

Stephen Bergman [16] refers to the concept of "relational dread," where emotional connection with others is feared and avoided. Dread arises from being in a relational process where complex things are happening quickly on both sides, a dynamic where one relational style (male) is meeting another quite different one (female). At issue is the process of relationship, not the person. A man's dread is the result of negative learning about the process of relationship, repeated over many years.

*"I have come to believe that the greatest liability of psychotherapy with a man is to reinforce a self-centered view of the world. Psychotherapy, especially those two methods that America fell so heavily in love with – self-psychology and psychoanalysis, can lead to a man delineating every nook and cranny of his inner landscape without having the faintest idea of what goes into being in mutual connection, in having a growth-fostering relationship with a woman or a man"* [17]

Overall, research has shown that Gender Role Conflict is often related to larger problems including depression, anxiety, relationship problems, low self-esteem, violence and a variety of other undesirable things. It is possible to reduce or minimize the negative effects of Gender Role Conflict by (a) recognizing it and (b) becoming more flexible in attitudes and behavior.

## Relational Dread and Codependency

Griffin and Dauer [18] linked the "male relationship dread" concept with Codependency in an incredibly articulate way. They note that "because men are taught to prize independence and are not taught the skills to develop interdependence, relationships become inherently threatening. As a man moves toward more intimacy and commitment in a relationship, he literally may experience dread as he faces the perceived loss of independence and is required to utilize skills he does not possess (and that have been systematically rejected as unmanly)." We must have authentic and mutual connection in relationships to grow and change. *Disconnection in relationships is the source of psychological problems.*

Griffin and Dauer suggest that skills such as fluency in the language of feelings, an ability to be vulnerable, a willingness to ask for and offer support, extending and honoring trust, compassion and empathy are rarely consistent with the "rules of being of a man" that boys are taught from a very early age. If we accept the notion that all human growth occurs through connection with others, then growing up male is a process that is inherently conflicted and perhaps even traumatic for many boys and young men.

> *When boys do not follow the expected rules and instead exhibit some of the qualities identified above as being necessary for intimate relationships, they are likely to suffer ridicule, shaming, alienation and even physical violence. Boys thus grow into men who lack the experience of learning and practicing relationship skills. And as men, they view intimacy and connection with fear and hostility. This is not because they do not desire intimacy and connection, but because they have little familiarity with them. In other words, men lack what we refer to as "relational competency."* [19]

Depending on the nature, frequency and relational context of the disconnections a person experiences with significant others in her or his life, and within the larger culture, these experiences can be accompanied by feelings of shame, fear, frustration, humiliation and self-blame. Jordan [20] stated that "shame is most importantly a felt sense of unworthiness to be in connection, a deep sense of unlovability, with the ongoing awareness of how very much one wants to connect with others" Disconnections that cannot be transformed have the potential to lead to feelings of condemned isolation.

*Feelings of deep shame about one's "neediness" and "lack of manly* virtues" become central to the internal experience of many boys and men. They may feel pride in their independence and self-sufficiency, but they also feel lonely and isolated, as well as emotionally and spiritually empty. There may develop a stark dissonance in how they present to others and how they feel inside. [21]

Men are disconnected from these internal feelings which are not permissible under the rules of being a man. However, this does not mean these feelings are not affecting the man and driving his behavior. Subsequently, men and their partners tend to focus on behaviors that take on the aspect of aggression, power and control while they ignore the underlying internal state. Some men might be constantly fighting an energy that pushes them toward extreme independence at the cost of their relationships. Other men are constantly fighting an energy that pushes them toward extreme dependence on others at the cost of their sense of self. Frequently, these opposing energies are driving behaviors in the same man at the same time.

## Conclusion I draw:

It is very likely that men who are more gender role identified would never be seen as codependent because so many of their gender role traits are "normal" for an avoidantly attached codependent. Men with gender role conflict may present as more anxious, in general, and are more likely to be identified as codependent. We will now examine how the symptoms of male codependency appear in men.

CHAPTER THREE

## *Symptoms of Codependency in Males*

### Symptom One: Lack of Attunement with Self

Avoiding awareness of our own reality is often an attempt to deny thoughts, desires or intentions we fear will threaten or contradict people with whom we feel strong attachment. We instinctively hide thoughts and feelings we assume would be threatening to other people and might cause them to leave us.

*Ken, 40 and Sandy, 36 have been married for ten years, with 4 year old male twins. Ken was raised in a chaotic military family, where his father would be deployed overseas for up to a year at a time, leaving him with his emotionally volatile mother. As an adolescent he promised himself he would never be in chaos again, and has refused to participate in conflict with women or co-workers his entire adult life. Ken deeply believes that once you allow conflict to enter a relationship separation is inevitable, consequently he is committed to "peace at all costs." Sandy has started to look for schools for the twins, anticipating Kindergarten for the next school year.*

*Sandy was educated as an elementary school teacher, and is a strong proponent of learning through exploration and play versus hard-core academics. Ken believes the world is based on competition, and is afraid his boys will be at a disadvantage if they are not taught competitive skills. He is afraid they may even be targeted by bullies as they grow older. Ken voices tentative objections to Sandy's plan, but abandons his attempts to influence her because it is "not worth" the conflict. In fact, he even agrees to participate in a parent co-op school that will demand more time than he had planned. He decides it is a necessary sacrifice for the good of the family, and jumps in.*

Sandy has no idea that Ken feels as strongly as he does. She would be surprised to hear him worry that objecting in any disruptive way would be a "deal breaker" in the relationship. In fact, she wishes Ken would participate more in decision making, often feeling the burden of making major family decisions on her own.

Ken's allegiance to Levant's restriction of emotions is in play in this vignette. Ken has adopted strong mechanisms to disengage from his discomfort as he agrees to Sandy's plans for his sons' education. No doubt, this is a mechanism learned early on as he was required to separate for long periods of time from his father and was left to cope with an intermittently available mother. Disengagement and relying on logic would be well within gender role "norms" as well as a strong symptom of Codependency.

Ken's gender role conflict would most likely be an internal one and increase strongly if he were pushed to be more assertive in his positions with Sandy. He would not recognize the attachment anxiety he experiences, and would most likely identify his fear of being a "different kind of man" than he identifies himself to be. This is a key reason healing at both an attachment level and gender role level would need to be addressed as each one could undermine attempts to heal the other.

Developmentally, we learn to be in tune with ourselves when we receive consistent, emotionally accurate responses from caregivers. Having our emotions accurately acknowledged teaches us an emotional vocabulary we can use to identify and share our internal emotional reality with others. However, if I grow up in a world where safety depends on reading my caregiver's emotions rather than my own, my internal world will remain a mystery to me.

Many of us find our internal worlds to be "beside the point." In fact, we are clueless about our external world as well, oblivious to our effects on others. When we lack an accurate internal observer we cannot self-correct and identify our blind spots. We also find ourselves unable to establish effective boundaries internally (our thoughts or feelings) or externally (our physical self and our possessions). Instead we are vulnerable to subtle and constant merging with those around us as we take on their emotions and their thoughts. We are vulnerable to the energetic influence of others, and our moods can be impacted and sharply shifted by changes in the people around us.

*Marvin has always believed that if you are in love, you should never have to ask for what you want and need. He believes that couples should always think in terms of "we" and idealizes relationships that seem to share everything. Marvin is in the separation and divorce process because his wife had an affair, though they are still living together until the financial details are settled and they can afford to live separately. In the meantime, Marvin has found his "soulmate" who understands his position and has agreed to enter a relationship even though he will not move out for three more months.*

*Marvin's girlfriend Jennifer has to attend a wedding and she knows she cannot invite him because it is on a weekend when he has his daughter and doesn't want to cause problems with his wife. Nonetheless he becomes incredibly angry when Jennifer tells him that she will be carpooling during the five hour trip with a male friend who is attending the wedding. He rants, "You are still thinking in terms of you! You didn't give a single thought to how I would feel about you spending so much time with another man. You are obviously not ready for a relationship if I am not your first concern. I guess I love more deeply than you do. Maybe we should break up!" he threatens.*

Marvin has no idea how unreasonable he sounds, and is completely disconnected from his own unavailability. He believes the only safe relationship is one in which they are completely "merged" and he can lose himself in his focus on Jennifer and her "intentions." Our lack of boundaries can be painfully obvious to everyone but us. We are so disconnected from our actual agendas, needs, and wants that we can be flabbergasted when someone makes note of our apparent lack of self.

## Symptom Two: Lack of Attunement with Others

All too frequently, anxiously attached codependents are missing a basic understanding of the thoughts and emotions of others. Lacking empathy, we have difficulty inferring or predicting the plans, intentions and motives of others... despite the fact we are always monitoring them to figure out how we should act!

This leads me to think about Codependents who crave attachment at one level, yet avoid intimacy at another. Due to our lack of internal attunement, even when we do connect with others it can feel somewhat unsatisfying – like one cookie. In fact, it's strange how we can believe we are so engaged while the Plexiglas between us and the other person remains staunchly intact. The vulnerability of being completely emotionally honest and exposed can be excruciatingly anxiety provoking. It creates anxiety for us when we are exposed, and creates anxiety for us when people around us are in pain. It is so much more comfortable to be DOING something, anything, rather than remaining in an exposed feeling state.

This unwillingness to be vulnerable (strongly supported by male gender role) leads us away from allowing others to support or take care of us. Our role is to anticipate the needs of others (thus earning our value), and more often than not others have no way to express their love to us by taking care of us. What if they find out we are "needy"? What if I find out I am "needy"?

*Jeremy has been raising his daughter Kara as a single parent since she was 4 years old. Kara's mother had disappeared into the drug culture years ago and Jeremy had always been worried about the effects of her mother's absence. If he was honest, he was afraid Kara would become an addict like her mother. Jeremy's own mother had married 4 times and by the age of 16 he was on his own. He identified with Kara's lack of maternal influence and had been focused on her welfare at the expense of his own for years.*

*Jeremy would say he knows Kara better than she knows herself. Lately, Jeremy is increasingly disturbed by the influence Kara's new boyfriend is having on her. He finds himself resisting her new "unladylike" desire to work on her car with him, and her strange new interest in vegetarianism. They have been barbecuing since Kara was a little girl, and her refusal to eat their favorite meals together has left him resentful and afraid. As Jeremy is becoming more irritable and critical, Kara is spending less and less time with him, and Jeremy is considering telling her she is on her own at 18 since she doesn't "need him" anymore.*

Jeremy clearly feels he is "losing control" over his daughter, and maintaining control is prominent both in his gender role and as a Codependent symptom. From an attachment perspective, Jeremy doesn't trust that his daughter values him as much as he values her, and he has worked for years to "earn" the love he now feels slipping away from him. He is convinced she can only love one person, rather than believing she has room to love multiple people. He can see he is "losing" to the new boyfriend, and his resulting anger and despair is creating the separation he most fears.

Two of Levant's gender role values (self-reliance and emotional detachment) contribute heavily to Jeremy's confusion. He sees his role as protector and provider, and if he follows through on his thoughts about placing Kara "on her own" he will experience tremendous gender role conflict. Jeremy's role as a provider has made him blind to Kara's growing confidence and esteem, so he blames the boyfriend for Kara's growth and changes. Maintaining his connection with Kara will require Jeremy to begin to see her individuation as a sign of positive parenting versus betrayal.

### Symptom Three: Distrusting the Attachment of others to the Codependent

People who are anxious or preoccupied with attachment frequently suspect that others don't value us as much as we value them. Often this is because we are over-giving and others cannot match our participation level. So, when we notice the discrepancy between our giving levels and theirs, we can develop resentments and interpret the imbalance as further proof that we are not "worthy" of being taken care of. It is proof of our foundational unloveability.

Our attempts to seek reassurance of our value and loveability can give us the appearance of neediness, with high levels of intensity due to emotional expressiveness and even impulsivity.

*Jose has been married to Angela for 8 tumultuous years. In this time, Angela has been in substance abuse treatment twice; once as a result of a family intervention and another time to beat a DUI charge. Jose "adores" Angela and truly believes if he meets her needs enough she will not "need" to drink. Jose has purchased two vehicles in the last three years for Angela due to car accidents. He has paid for an attorney and a bail bondsman, as well as mandated DUI programs. He paid for two private rehabilitation facilities, afraid of the class of people she might meet in a county program. Jose has participated in the family programs during both treatment episodes, and has been exposed to terms like "boundary setting" and the family systems effects of drinking.*

*Angela is finishing her second treatment episode and the program is suggesting that she transition to a Sober Living Home. Jose is horrified by this idea, "What kind of man puts his wife on the street?" Jose feels others will not be as available or as supportive as he would be and he would do a "better job" monitoring her structure and getting her to her aftercare meetings on time. Jose is shocked to learn that the Sober Living Home is Angela's idea, and feels betrayed by her desire to "leave him." Jose storms out of her discharge planning meeting, "Fine. You want to be away from me – you got it!"*

Jose obviously feels strongly about his role as a protector and provider, and is heavily invested in "earning" his wife's love and appreciation. Jose demonstrates Levant's rule of being self-reliant. He is in denial of his own "need" and "dependence" on his wife, instead focusing on his belief about her need for him. He also exemplifies Levant's rule to make achievement the top priority and fully expects his efforts on Angela's behalf to create the merging he is unconsciously seeking. Yet despite this expectation he finds the idea of a merger terrifying, so he picks a partner incapable of meeting his need for merger leaving him frustrated and resentful "after all he does" for her.

Jose strongly identifies with traditional gender role values. Consequently, he finds ideas like "giving his wife more room to find herself" and "encouraging her to depend on a sponsor (outsider)" extremely distasteful. They contradict his image of himself as a man. His male role is heavily entwined with his attachment issues, and sorting through the overlap will take an experienced counselor who can help Jose see his behaviors more clearly. Saving his relationship will require him to tolerate some gender role conflict and he will need support to tolerate his attachment anxiety as well.

Codependents frequently feel a strong need to "earn" the attachment of others, distrusting that their presence, who they are, will be enough. We over-extend, over-give, and seem to be always operating from a deficit position. It is as though we are "making up for" everything we are not. We notice that other people do not seem to extend this much energy into their relationships, which is puzzling because we don't see it as optional. For us, over-achieving is "required" to secure attachments from people we love, even though we never really trust the attachment since it's based on what we do rather than who we are. Men often feel victimized by trying to be a "nice guy," and wonder if they should be a "bigger prick" because other people seem to respond to this more passionately!

*Tony has been dating John for the last 9 months and has been a successful software designer for the last 8 years. John is completing his licensure hours as a marriage and family therapist and has begun to build a small practice. He has been living on financial aid and is worried about finding supplementary employment as he continues to build his practice. Tony has been quietly watching John's progress and has begun to lose sleep, worrying about John's situation. Tony feels enormous internal pressure to provide for John even though his own financial situation is tenuous due to bad investments. John has never asked him for help but Tony decides to ask John to move in with him to make John's financial situation easier.*

*Tony makes this suggestion to John but does not mention his own anxiety as a motivator. He allows John to believe this is a romantic proposal, and John is excited that the relationship is moving forward. John is acutely aware of the financial discrepancy in their earnings and has tried to raise this topic multiple times hoping to be clear about the expectations they have of each other. Tony evades this topic for months until the afternoon John brings home organic groceries, at which point Tony loses his mind and starts listing all the ways he is "bailing John out." John is devastated by this accusation.*

Tony does not question his "responsibility" to take care of John, and even projects onto John the expectation he will financially provide. Tony is the oldest of 5 children raised by an addicted gambler father and struggling, anxious mother. Tony began working to help the family at the age of 12 when his uncle hired him to work in his butcher shop. This allowed Tony to make money and also to bring home meat to the family every week. Tony adored his Uncle, the opposite of his irresponsible father and believed that being a "man" like his Uncle meant adapting what Levant would call restricted emotions, self-reliance, avoiding the feminine, even homophobia. Tony's internalized homophobia exaggerated his fear of being female or subordinate, so interdependence with another man was not an option to Tony. He would experience terrific role conflict if he were to expect or allow John to participate equally, seeing this as being "weak" or "needy." Tony's disengagement from his emotions and physical self means that he is unaware of how exhausted he is, having worked since he was 12, and how much he would love to share his burden. Tony does not see this is an option.

Like many men, Tony believes he will only be loved is he does the heavy lifting in the relationship. He doesn't expect a fair exchange, and is surprised when he gets resentful. Anxious codependents instinctively resent people who "get away" with acting poorly or unequally in a relationship and don't seem to lose the attachment. They seem to have more permission and freedom in their relationships than the codependent. It is confusing and frustrating for us to work so hard in our lives without success, and then to see "chosen" others who enjoy continued attachments yet don't (in our opinion) appear to deserve them.

When you are secure in your relationships, and trust other's attachment to you, it is natural to expect that your relationships will be mutual. It will be uncomfortable for you if they are not. It would be weird if you let someone give way more to you than you give to them, and visa versa. Over time, you want the give and take to be easy and balanced. You want to be "self-supporting by your own contributions" as we say in recovery, but we also place service and unity in very high regard. I wonder what it was like for John to be on the receiving end of Tony's martyrdom?

The misplaced grandiosity is hard to see when you are earning your value. It feels like "love" to be so self-sacrificing and take on the burden - giving others a pass to not fully participate as an equal. In fact, we rarely treat people like equals – no one else can be trusted to take care of things correctly; to make sure everything is done "right." How can someone with such low self-esteem feel like they are the only competent person in the world? It's truly amazing!

When we see how all our work has failed to secure the loyalty and consistent responsiveness we have tried so hard to earn, the resentment is painful and overwhelming. Even more so when we notice others getting it seemingly without effort. We blame ourselves, and sometimes feel victimized by others.

## Symptom Four: Escalation to protect attachment

In this symptom, manipulation is used to keep the inattentive or inconsistent partner involved by alternating dramatic angry demands with needy dependence, the gender role identified men will be in denial of this needy aspect of the cycle. When the partner is preoccupied and not paying attention, the anxious Codependent explodes in angry demands and behaviors that cannot be ignored.

The partner either reacts with hostility, punishing the codependent, or with sympathy, rewarding the manipulation. This cycle can develop into patterns of responding to hostility with sweetness and dependency, and responding to sympathy with anger and new demands. The two are enmeshed together in a never-ending cycle of dissatisfaction.

Codependents can be emotionally volatile adults who seek reassurance, but find only partial and temporary soothing from contact with significant people in our lives. Our inability to self-soothe and regulate our emotions creates a need for external calming solutions (including vulnerability to substance abuse) to address our emotional distress.

*Alex has been worried about his wife, Becky, who has been changing since she turned forty. Last month she announced that she had enrolled in school to finish her bachelor's degree in accounting now that the children are more independent. She has class three mornings and one night each week, and is insisting on "study time" during the weekend. Alex is confused about this change, believing this is a message to him that he's not making enough money. He is beginning to feel resentful and criticized. If Alex was more self-aware, he might recognize deep fears around the possibility Becky will be influenced by new people she meets in school, maybe even another man.*

*However Alex is not aware he feels threatened by Becky's schooling, consequently he begins to point out ways in which the children and family are no longer her priority. It is common for Alex to become argumentative with Becky before her evening class and she consistently finds herself weepy and distracted on the way to school, fearful that maybe she really is being "self-ish" and hurting her family. Things finally come to head one night when Alex arrives home the night of class and finds that Becky is finishing a paper and there is no meal prepared. Alex immediately feels dismissed and unimportant. He responds with escalating anger and accusations. He gives Becky an ultimatum – stay home or move out!*

I am reminded of our discussion of Levant's rule of focus on toughness and aggression. And also the possibility that Donovan has described: Alex is having adrenal reactions prompted by the feeling his self-image being threatened. His sympathetic nervous system erupts and he is hijacked by his fight or flight response. He and Becky are interpreting this reaction as anger when in fact there is no real offense taking place. Rather, Alex feels dismissed, disrespected and devalued. He is interpreting his wife's ambitions as gender role devaluation, a perspective which escalates his response.

Alex is in denial about his own dependence and neediness. He sees himself as operating in Levant's "self-reliant" standard and feels his role as an achiever and provider is under attack, justifying his reactivity. Sadly, Alex is creating the very distance from his wife he fears school attendance will bring, and he remains oblivious to his role in threatening the attachment. If he had been able to tolerate the gender role conflict and simply trust Becky, he would be closer to the interdependence he craves.

When anxious codependents become triggered our frontal lobe decision making often gets shut down. Limbic system arousal hijacks our reasoning, resulting in a fight or flight response. It is important to keep in mind how the adrenalin response to fear often cripples our ability respond from a rational, grown-up perspective. We strike out in ways that ultimately injure others (and our relationships), not to mention our self-esteem.

In her book, Facing Codependence, Pia Mellody points out the "lack of moderate" is one of the most obvious signs of codependency to others. Moderation is essentially a self-containment issue and is related to both boundary and reality issues. When an individual has no boundaries with which to contain himself, he will do whatever he wants to do, disregarding his impact on others. He loses control of being in control of himself and others. In this process, he may attempt to control by being out of control and others will have difficulty being rational.

*Edward had been a police officer for ten years, and married for five years. His wife, Karen, is 10 years younger and Edward is crazy about her. His first wife refers to her as "the bimbo." He knows Karen tends to be impulsive in her decision making but her spontaneity provides a welcome contrast to his own instinctive caution and he feels grateful that this joyful woman is in his life.*

*Lately Edward is having trouble reaching Karen during the day. She is a real estate open house staging expert and her schedule is flexible. Karen is not tech savvy, so she is unaware that Edward has taken the precaution of activating her GPS. Edward tells himself it's "just in case there is an emergency" and he needs to reach her. He also put her on his phone plan so he can check who she is calling by reviewing their bill on-line. Edward has stopped telling Karen about his shift changes, "surprising" her and then expecting her to shift her schedule to spend time with him. If Karen doesn't shift her schedule, Edward either invites himself to go along or pouts the rest of the day, refusing to interact when she gets home. Edward does not see himself as controlling but rather protective, which he believes is his role is a man.*

Boundaries are hard to set and maintain when you have anxious or avoidant attachment issues. Setting boundaries with ourselves and others can feel like we are betraying or endangering the attachment. Pia Mellody points out that boundaries serve to both contain and protect, which is always a revolutionary thought for good codependents. We focus instead on our need to set limits on others, not letting them "victimize" us anymore. One of the more painful reality checks we face is recognizing that frequently these others need protection from us! WE are the problem more often than we like to admit. When driven by anxiety and a need to be right, we give ourselves permission to invade the space of others. After all, we know we LOVE them and only want what's best for them.

Any committed Codependent has thought at least once in their life, "If they would just do what I tell them, everything would be fine." It's a male gender role requirement to be "right" and know the answer, so rejection of our information can feel like a personal rejection. We repeat ourselves so often not because we like to nag but because if you don't do what we "suggest" we assume you didn't hear us. Because if you heard and understood what we were telling you, you would naturally CHOOSE to take our advice. But don't worry, we'll tell you again… and again, and again.

The painful part of this scenario is the pain we feel when you don't do what we suggest, or don't listen to us. We believe we have little to offer aside from solving your problem solutions and doing things for you. Consequently, when our offer is rejected, it goes into the "See, I'm not worth shit" pile and challenges our contribution to the relationship. We are always finding evidence of this, and unfortunately we tend to gravitate towards people who will provide us with plenty of this kind of dismissive evidence.

This escalation – or striking out behavior – is so young, isn't it? How old is it to have a tantrum, or tell Mommy "I hate you!" just to wound her? When I look at Codependent behavior I so often see the arrested emotional development that doesn't match our external competence. We are so accomplished in so many ways – over responsible and smart. How is it that such an articulate, accomplished man is suddenly hurling words across the room like a four year old? "I want a new Mommy!" From the outside, the powerlessness of this approach is painfully obvious. But from the inside it is only painful.

There is no organized problem solving thought in this behavior. There is no taking of personal responsibility for our choices. There is only acting out in response to the excruciating limbic arousal we feel when our relational well being is threatened.

## Symptom Five: Denial of Dependency or Attachment Needs

John Bowlby pointed out that developmentally, it is important to be able to return to our attachment figure for comfort in the face of perceived threat or discomfort. For avoidant codependents, the caregiver was most likely not able or willing to consistently comfort, and may have even been punishing when comfort was requested.

We may have been ridiculed or shamed for requiring reassurance or for having negative emotions about the caregiver. It is possible our caregivers could not tolerate the expression of any negative emotions whatsoever, and may even have threatened abandonment – "You could always just go live somewhere else," or "So get a new mommy if you don't like the one you have!"

Some of us may have simply been ignored when expressing our needs, and we became fiercely self-reliant to avoid the pain of neglect or non-responsiveness. Ultimately we become our own secure base, distrusting the capacity of others to provide our needs. We become counter-dependent – if I can't fulfill a need for myself, then I will do without.

We will not risk possible rejection or non-response when asking for help, a position which is supported and reinforced in gender role conformity. If we are forced into accepting assistance, we will feel obligated to return the help ten-fold. We assume assistance always comes with strings attached and we are unwilling to be placed in such a vulnerable position. It is unacceptable to "need" others in any tangible, structural way. It would be "unmanly."

*Craig has been working with the marketing team at a software company for the last four years. His colleagues would describe him as competent, helpful and reliable. He is a trusted member of the team. The company is preparing to launch a new project, which means that the marketing team is working closely with PR and they are working many extra hours as the launch gets closer. John has been worried for the last two months about his level of fatigue, and he noticed a small mass in his groin area two weeks ago. Unbeknownst to his team, he has been squeezing in doctors' visits during his lunch hour to avoid inconveniencing anyone else. His doctor is supposed to call him with his biopsy results in the next two days, and Craig is having an even harder time sleeping.*

*His team members notice that Craig is "off his game" and ask him if everything is alright. Craig reassures them he is fine, no more tired and stressed than they are. He returns to his project and begins working, anxious that others are "noticing" a change in his performance and terrified of the judgment he assumes they are passing on his performance. He doesn't hear their concern – he assumes only criticism and judgment. He drinks extra coffee, keeps working to "make up" for the weakness they observed and does not confide in anyone.*

Craig is operating out of Levant's rules of being self-reliant, focusing on toughness, and focus on achievement. He is using tremendous energy to remain detached from the pain he may be feeling physically as well as his exhaustion. Craig ignores the anxiety that is disturbing his sleep, tries not to let his medical care inconvenience others, and doesn't recognize the support and affection his co-workers are offering him. He is too intent on avoiding the judgment that his "neediness" could provoke.

A quick overview of Craig's history would reveal an absent father and single mother who worked two jobs to support Craig and his brother. Craig's mother was often exhausted and depressed from her husband's abandonment. She would often drink in the evening to fall asleep. Craig learned early that the best way to gain approval was to be as independent as possible, take care of himself and his little brother and be quiet in the evening after his mother had headed off to bed. Craig's mother would brag about her "little man." She was grateful that he was so self-sufficient, unlike his demanding little brother who made their mom even more distressed and tired than she normally was.

Craig would not only experience tremendous gender role conflict if he were to attempt greater openness with others, but it would also challenge his avoidant attachment patterns. In order for Craig to begin to have more satisfying relationships he will definitely need to link his role expectations with his behavior in relationships. He must also break through his emotional and physical disengagement to honestly face his sadness and loneliness.

Avoidant codependents learn early in life that the parent experiences their presence as intrusive or demanding. Shortly thereafter they become self-sufficient in order to avoid being perceived as a "bother" and the rejection that entails.

*Roger had met his colleague, Sandra, several times over the last few years at various professional conferences. They struck up a comfortable friendship and clearly enjoyed each other's company. Roger was keenly aware that Sandra was married, largely because Sandra was increasingly candid about her frequent loneliness and lack of marital satisfaction. One afternoon after a couple glasses of wine, Sandra went back to Roger's room and the two of them had a wonderful evening. In the morning, Roger looked over at the sleeping Sandra and felt his heart begin to race. He was panicked about "what would happen next." Roger was angry at himself because he had fostered their closeness with nearly daily personal phone calls as Sandra's confidant, and yet he had only been comfortable in this role because she was married!*

*As much as he was drawn to Sandra and enjoyed her, he had the sinking feeling that if they ever attempted an "actual" relationship she would quickly tire of him and leave. When Sandra woke up, Roger was already dressed and quickly informed her that his flight had been changed to return home later that morning. While he could see the confusion and hurt in her eyes, he told himself, "Its better this way," and did not return Sandra's calls for the next week.*

Obviously Roger is way more comfortable with the marriage buffer between them. He abandons Sandra before taking the risk of developing a relationship that might fail. Roger is more than willing to extend intimacy as long as there is a built-in firewall!

Roger is comfortable in his avoidant attachment pattern, which includes Levant's gender role rule of non-relational sexuality. Roger is far more comfortable providing advice, offering suggestions and even performing sexually. None of these functions place him at risk to violate Levant's "self-reliant" rule, exposing him as "needy" or "dependent." Roger may be in touch with his aloneness but believes it is inevitable due not only to his gender role but also to his avoidant attachment style. Roger will need to challenge both belief systems in order to achieve true intimacy.

Avoidant codependents are often oblivious to the detached messages they give to others, even those they would describe as "intimate" others. While men very much want to be needed (increasing the reliability of attachments from others), they remain careful to protect themselves from revealing any "neediness" or "dependence" they may have in a relationship.

## Symptom Six: Avoiding Intimacy

When others attempt to penetrate our self-reliance we can exhibit a variety of self-protective mechanisms designed to "appear" intimate when we are not, or participate in "counterfeit emotional involvement." With intimacy comes the possibility of "engulfment" or being taken hostage by the demands of others. Our perceptions of the "demands" and obligations placed upon us by those who claim to love us may be distorted. Trusting love to be unconditional is almost impossible and we are always scanning for the unstated "subtext" or hidden "agenda" connected to this love.

Our fear is that we will allow ourselves to become "dependent" on someone for structure and support, only to experience the abandonment or non-response our "internal working models" tell us is inevitable. We invest a certain amount of "pride" in our ability to maintain our "self-sufficiency." This pride may extend to refusing to allow others to give to us, rejecting their offers of presents or dinner invitations to avoid the "tab" we expect to pay at a later time.

*Leonard was visiting his grandfather for the summer, and as much as he enjoyed his grandfather's company, he wondered why his grandfather had very few phone calls. His grandfather did play pool and one afternoon one of his pool player buddies called and invited Leonard and his grandfather for brunch on Sunday. Leonard watched as his grandfather hung up the phone and began to be agitated and uneasy. When Leonard asked about this, his grandfather stated, "They probably just want us to come over and help them move something. If I accept then I'll get roped into something because there's no such thing as a "free lunch." I'll be obligated to have them over, and my apartment isn't set up to entertain. I don't know what they really want." Leonard was startled by his grandfather's perspective and suggested that it was possible that they simply wanted to have them to brunch because they liked him! This caused his grandfather to "snort" in response, wagging his head at Leonard's naiveté.*

*Leonard had recently left a substance abuse treatment center and was staying with his Grandfather while he got back on his feet. Leonard had always loved his Grandfather and hoped to be of more help now that he was clean and sober. He realized after this conversation that it was quite possible his*

*Grandfather did not trust Leonard's affection for him either, assuming that he was just "using him" for a place to stay.*

*Leonard began to struggle with shame as he considered this idea. Fortunately he decided to call his sponsor for support.*

Leonard comes from a multi-generational male structure deeply committed to Levant's rules of gender role. Clearly, Leonard has to challenge his own uneasiness and risk feeling gender role conflict from others as his grandfather would not support his relationship with his sponsor. Grandfather's advice would be to "man up" and handle his business. To be self-reliant and maintain the same restricted emotional state the Grandfather himself had adopted his entire life.

Leonard's grandfather is quite possibly glad to have Leonard's company but would never acknowledge this to himself. His self-image as a male requires him to see his motivation as helping or providing rather than admitting his need or dependency on Leonard.

**Where does this fear of being trapped (or needing to take hostages and trap others) come from?**

Developmental theorists would say we are connecting attachment with engulfment. So, if I love you, you will pull up to me with a U-Haul and take me over, or if I love you I will pull up to you with a U-Haul and lose myself in you. We don't have the tools to remain independent and still connected. We don't know how to share power. The people we love would be really uneasy if they knew how many Plan B's we have. Ironically enough, we have back-up plans because we expect THEM to leave or things to "not work out."

## Symptom Seven: Walls Instead of Boundaries

If our compensating style is one of compulsive anticipation of other's needs, we can appear to be more accessible that we actually are. We are often highly available to others while being careful to not "burden" others with our issues. We avoid allowing ourselves to express any "need" for comfort from people who may fail us or be unresponsive. In fact, we may have "Teflon coating." The disappointments and heartaches of life appear to have no impact upon us. We simply persevere in the face of challenges. It never occurs to us to ask for assistance.

If we need to have the couch moved, we will find a way to move it ourselves. If we are ill, we go the store, get our own medication and chicken soup and hole up in our home until we are "fit" to return to the world with our image intact.

Anne Wilson Schaef refers to this as "impression management." We invest a great deal of energy into managing the feelings and impressions of others. If we are honest with ourselves, very few people actually "know us" at an intimate level, though they may have the impression they are closer to us than they are. In fact, people who love us would be surprised by how little we trust them or expect them to be available to us, and by how vigilant we are for signs of impending disloyalty or abandonment. We always have an exit plan ready for the "inevitable" broken attachment. This justifies withholding parts of our selves.

If we have a grandiose streak, we may even begin to believe our own image, and see ourselves as super-competent. We may judge others, albeit silently, for their weakness in letting themselves get dependent on others then "broken" when the relationship is disrupted.

Have you ever judged someone as "weak" for admitting needing someone else?

*Michael had been working with Frank for several years at the company. They were hired in the same month, and bonded together as they learned the company culture. They had been supporters and colleagues. Frank would have called Michael his closest friend. Frank fell in love with a woman in marketing and, against company policy, began a relationship with her that put both of their jobs at risk. Michael was aghast at Frank's foolishness. He could feel himself recoil as Frank tried to explain his passion for this woman, his sense that he had met someone who truly had his back, someone with whom he could see spending the rest of his life. Internally Michael rolled his eyes and began to lose respect for Frank for placing himself in an increasingly vulnerable position.*

*At one point, Frank let down his guard and his boss saw him making out in the car with the woman from marketing. Frank and the woman were called in by human resources and fired for unprofessional conduct. As painful as this was, Frank still felt he had come out ahead because he "got the girl." Frank was shocked as Michael abandoned the friendship, disgusted by Frank's poor priorities. In Michael's worldview you should never give other people the power to affect your life in such important ways. Frank genuinely thought Michael cared as much about him as he cared about Michael.*

If we knew more about Michael, we would know that his relationship history includes being extremely careful to never allow his partners to be equal financially or even to be on the lease at his condominium. When he makes the decision to live with someone, they are required to move in with him so that when the relationship ends he will not have his housing situation disrupted. He always knows he can afford expenses on his own. Truthfully, it is hard to buy him gifts because when he needs or wants something he simply goes and gets it. It never occurs to him to wait and allow someone else to provide it for him.

Michael also represents Levant's rules of self-reliance, focus on achievement and avoidance of being feminine. Perhaps also being non-relational about sexuality. Michael would say that Frank was "pussy whipped" and would never let his life be controlled by feelings instead of logic. Gender role conformity suggests that logic is always superior to feelings and being logical is connected to remaining independent. Frank experiences some gender role devaluation from Michael as he experienced Michael's judgment and withdrawal due to his choices.

**Levant's Principles also provide multiple familiar male "walls."**

**For example:**

- The man hiding in the garage nights and weekends "puttering" about with the bounty of Craftsman tools he receives on every occasion.
- The man who comes home, has dinner and stays absorbed in the television all night to "relax" while polishing off several bottles of beer.

- The man who carries an "angry vibe" like a shield, always ready to erupt at perceived disrespect or injustice.

- The man who sleeps poorly, worried about finances and college funds, so stays on the computer long after everyone has gone to sleep.

- The man who rarely speaks, rarely offers input, who sees himself as a "good listener" though tuned out.

- The man who begins endless large projects around the house, making him unavailable for family outings.

- The man who is coaching multiple sports teams, making him unavailable to spend quality time with his own children.

- The high achiever who is away on endless "road trips" necessary to "provide for the family."

- The man who is highly committed to his church, volunteering on multiple committees and making home visits 2 or 3 nights a week to parishioners.

- The man who uses walls of words, endlessly issuing commands, directives, giving unrequested advice and admonishments. Men I think of as "the mouth" - they weigh in on every decision or thought a family member has.

CHAPTER FOUR

## *Codependency as a Chronic Stress Disorder*

### Codependency as a Chronic Stress Disorder

Recall the last part of our Codependency definition:

*Ultimately, Codependency is a chronic stress disease, which can devastate our immune system and lead to systemic and even life-threatening illness.*

The longer I work with codependent men the more frequently I see the physical damage that comes from years of relational stress. Male physical self-neglect is part of Levant's Principles, and the combination of relationship stress, attachment distrust and poor self-care inevitably fore-shortens life span. The physical damage of Codependency makes addressing this issue and imperative! Our minds and bodies are inseparable... even if we spend most of our time walking around like "floating heads," unaware we are not inhabiting our bodies. There is plenty of research linking early attachment disruption and illness, and I have added a few examples at the end of this chapter to help you understand this critical connection in greater depth.

### Physical Consequences of Male Gender Role Stress

Male Gender Role Stress refers to emotional distress resulting directly from violating or not adhering to traditional masculine gender role norms.

*Lonnie is the 27 year old son of a third generation electrician, and work throughout his childhood to develop the skills the other men in the family had. His father and uncles were hard workers, had a good reputation with the community, and took pride in providing well for their families. Looking back, Lonnie can see how once he hit high school he made every possible mistake he could make. In an effort to create his own identity, he skipped classes, ran with a "fast" crowd, and was the first in the family to be arrested. In fact, he is the first to be "addicted" to alcohol and drugs, when*

everyone else appears to manage their drinking. He has been avoiding family occasions for years, deeply ashamed of his "weakness," and even more
ashamed that he has not met any of the standards of being an adult male
that the other men in the family demonstrate.

**Problems Linked to Male Gender Role Stress**

Simply put, men experiencing male gender role stress are more likely to
manifest anxiety, depression, difficulty controlling aggressive behavior and
alcohol abuse. Male gender role stress may also prevent many men from
seeking social support or using other healthy coping skills. For example,
men who fear violating male gender role norms are less likely to explore
or express their emotions, especially emotions which suggest vulnerability,
such as sadness or anxiety.

Less simply (but more thoroughly) put, here are some of the research findings upon which this conclusion is based. It's dense reading, but only a page
or two:

Masculine gender-role stress (MGRS) refers to the cognitive appraisal of a
specific situation as being stressful for men.[22] MGRS is a theoretical construct that describes the stress experienced by men when they feel they
are not meeting culturally sanctioned masculine gender-role behavior or
when the situation forces men to act in stereotypically feminine ways.[23]
The pressure men tend to place on themselves reflects stressful experiences around (a) physical inadequacy, (b) emotional inexpressiveness (c)
subordination to women, (d) intellectual inferiority, and (e) performance
failure. Masculine gender role stress (as measured by the Masculine Gender Role Stress Scale [MGRSS]) predicted increased anger, anxiety,[24] and
hostility.[25] It has also been found to relate to type-A coronary-prone behavior and elevated blood pressure.[26] Masculine gender role stress was
also found to be associated with failing to engage in health promoting behaviors[27] and with risky health habits.[28-29]

In a study of the relationship between scores on masculine gender role
stress and blood pressure reactivity, men exposed to the cold pressor
test (in which hands are submerged in ice cold water) were given either
neutral instructions (in which they were told they were simply providing

physiological data) or masculine challenge instructions (in which they were told that exposure of their hands in ice cold water was a measure of strength, endurance and ability to withstand pain). For men in the masculine challenge group, large differences in reactivity were found, with high-scoring MGRSS men showing higher reactivity (greater increases in blood pressure). No differences were found between men in the neutral instruction group.[30]

Accumulated evidence supports the view that the way men are traditionally socialized to be masculine can have hazardous mental and physical health consequences.[31] For example, gender-role conflict has been shown to be related to men's overall psychological distress;[32] lower self-esteem and higher anxiety;[33] higher levels of anger and substance use;[34] a higher level of depression;[35] and sexual aggression against women.[36] Research on masculine gender-role stress shows similar results in that gender-role stress has been reported to be associated with problematic behaviors, negative emotions, anger, and hostility as well as elevated blood pressure and high-risk health habits.[37,38] Social constructionists also relate gender-role conflict and stress to a higher likelihood of men committing suicide than women.[39] The line of reasoning in this approach is that men's "gender identity" is subsumed by an overall "dominant " and that it results in men's being unable to seek help.[40] More specifically, men do not usually talk about their problems to anyone out of fear or embarrassment of being seen as weak (i.e., it would not be considered manly). In addition, the relative loss of status experienced by men produces a social, psychological, and economic climate that is conducive to an increase in men's suicide.[41]

CHAPTER FIVE

## *Physiology of the Stress Response Connected to Codependency and Male Gender Role Stress*

### Physiology of the Stress Response Connected to Codependency and Male Gender Role Stress

Understanding how the nervous system responds to stress is essential in explaining stress-related diseases and conditions created by the chronic systemic drain of codependency and gender role conflict. Attachment issues set the emotional and developmental stage for these issues, and strong adherence to Levant's rules increases our vulnerability. But the fight or flight response is the actual mechanism which leads to our physical deterioration and compromised immune system. The fight or flight response prepares us to respond to an emergency. Masculine Gender Role Stress can create a constant stream of perceived emergencies. Each time a man faces a threat to his gender role identity a sympathetic nervous system response is triggered (this stress revs his body's engine way up into the red zone). When this reaction is turbocharged by early attachment disruption, he is pushing an overwrought system closer to the breaking point.

### The Alarm Reaction

The human body and human mind each have a set of very important and very predictable responses to threat. Threat may come from external sources (e.g. an attacker) or internal sources (e.g. unmotivated worries & fears). For Codependents, fear of abandonment is triggering. In male gender role stress, the pressure men tend to place on themselves reflects stressful experiences around (a) physical inadequacy, (b) emotional inexpressiveness, (c) subordination to women, (d) intellectual inferiority and (e) performance failure. One common reaction to danger or threat has been labeled the "fight or flight" reaction. In the initial stages of this reaction, there is a response called the alarm reaction

Think about what happens when you feel threatened. Your racing heart, sweaty palms, nausea and sense of impending harm are all symptomatic of this alarm reaction.

During a traumatic event, all aspects of the individual's functioning change, including feeling, thinking and behaving. For instance, someone under direct assault abandons thoughts of the future or abstract plans for survival. At that exact moment, all of the victim's thinking, behaving and feeling is being directed by more primitive parts of the brain.

A frightened child in a threatening situation doesn't focus on the words being spoken; instead, he or she is busy attending to the threat-related signals in their environment.

The fearful child will key in to nonverbal signs of communication, cues such as:

- eye contact
- facial expression
- body posture
- proximity to the threat

The internal state of the child also shifts with the level of *perceived* threat. As the level of threat increases (either real or perceived), a child moves along the arousal continuum from vigilance to terror.

These changes in the central nervous system cause hypervigilance. Under threat, the child tunes out all non-critical information. These actions prepare the child to do battle with or run away from the potential threat.

## DISSOCIATION (Freeze)

The fight-or-flight response is a well-characterized reaction to danger as we've already discussed. A second common reaction pattern to threat is dissociation. Dissociation is the mental mechanism by which one withdraws attention from the outside world and focuses on the inner world.

Because of their small size and limited physical capabilities, young children do not usually have the fight-or-flight option in a threatening situation. When fighting or physically fleeing is not possible, the child may use avoidant and psychological freezing mechanisms that are categorized as dissociative.

Dissociation due to threat and/or trauma may involve:
- a distorted sense of time.

- a detached feeling that you are observing something happening to you as if it is unreal -- the sense that you are watching a movie of your life.

- in extreme cases, children may withdraw into an elaborate fantasy world where they assume special powers or strengths.

Like the alarm response, this "defeat" or dissociative response happens along a continuum. The intensity of the dissociation varies with the intensity and duration of the traumatic event. Actually, we use dissociative mechanisms all the time, even when we are not threatened. Daydreaming is an example. However, during a traumatic event all children and most adults engage some higher degree of dissociation; the unreal sense that you are watching yourself, for instance. In fact, some individuals use dissociation so frequently it becomes their primary response mechanism.

For most children and adults the adaptive response to an acute trauma involves a mixture of hyperarousal and dissociation. During the actual trauma, the child feels threatened and the arousal systems will activate. As the threat increases, the child moves along the continuum into hyperarousal. At some point the dissociative response is activated, launching a host of protective mental responses (decreased perception of anxiety and pain) and physiological responses (decreased heart rate). Now the hyperarousal system can begin to slow down.

Today we know the body cannot tell the difference between an emotional emergency and physical danger. When triggered, it responds to either situation by pumping out stress chemicals designed to impel someone to flee to safety or stand and fight. In the case of childhood problems, where the family itself has become the source of significant stress, there may be no opportunity to fight or flee. For many children, the only perceived option is to freeze and shut down their inner responses by numbing or withdrawing into a fantasy world.

When young children are frightened into fight, flight or freeze they have no way of assessing the level of threat or using reason to modulate their reaction. The brain's limbic system becomes frozen in a fear response.

The only way out is for a caring adult to hold, reassure, and restore the child to a state of equilibrium which is available if a secure attachment with the caregiver exists. When primary caregivers are not available to soothe and reassure, the child is left to the fight, flight or freeze system without support.

### Why is the Fight or Flight Response Important?

Understanding the sympathetic and parasympathetic nervous system response to stress is important in explaining stress-related diseases and conditions created by the chronic stress of codependency. While attachment issues set the emotional and developmental stage for future behaviors, the fight or flight response is the physical mechanism that leads to our physiological deterioration and weakened immune system. The fight or flight response (named by Cannon and Selye in the 1930s) is a pattern of physiological responses that prepare us to respond to an emergency.

In the animal kingdom the rules are simple - only the strong survive. When faced with danger, the two main options are fighting (when you perceive the enemy to be weak or when defending your cubs/territory), and running away (when you encounter a huge hungry lion, for example). In the face of danger the body shifts immediately into high physiological arousal which enables fight or flight. This is designed as a short-term response to threat and the level of arousal is supposed to settle within a short period of time – after the lion is gone.

*I emphasize two points about this healthy stress response: First, it takes priority over all other metabolic functions. Second, it wasn't designed to last very long.*

So, how is fighting a lion related to anxiety about an upcoming meeting with our employer? Our physical response to a perceived threat is EXACTLY the same. When our attachment issues are triggered, we respond exactly as though it was a lion. However, rather than an occasional lion visit – maybe every three months – we perceive threats to our attachment repeatedly;

sometimes several times a day. And each time we do, we experience intense adrenal system arousal and release cortisol (the "rust" of the human body). This is *bad*. Let me explain...

First, let's look at how the Autonomic Nervous System (ANS) responds to threat and how that translates into physical damage over time.

The ANS is responsible for many functions in the body that occur "automatically" such as digestion, heart rate, blood pressure, and body temperature. The activity of the autonomic nervous system takes place completely beneath our conscious control. It is automatic.

There are two branches of the ANS designed to regulate the fight-or-flight response: the sympathetic and parasympathetic system. The sympathetic nervous system is the part of the ANS responsible for initiating the fight-or-flight response. Each time we have a thought of danger or pain, the sympathetic nervous system rings the alarm, initiating the fight-or-flight response and preparing us to handle potential danger or pain. It's an automatic reaction. As soon as we *believe* we're in danger a flood of physiological and emotional activity launches, instantly increasing our power, speed, and strength. The word "believe" is key here, because it means you don't have to actually threaten to leave me, I can merely picture you leaving me and I still get launched!

The other branch of the autonomic nervous system is called the parasympathetic nervous system. This branch is designed to bring us back to homeostasis (normal functioning) after the threat, danger or potential pain no longer seems imminent. Homeostasis is a state of internal stability of our physiology and our emotions. The function of the parasympathetic nervous system is to slow things down, to return us to a calmer state. During parasympathetic activity, blood concentrates in the central organs for digestion and storage of energy reserves. Breathing slows, as does heart rate. Blood pressure and body temperature drop. In general, muscle tension decreases. During parasympathetic activity (general relaxation) we are quiet and calm. The body regenerates and prepares for future activity.

The autonomic nervous system is controlled by the hypothalamus, which is commonly known as the "master gland." The hypothalamus receives the message of danger from the higher-order thinking component of the mind and uses the nervous system to trigger alarms in every other bodily system. The hypothalamus also delivers a message to the endocrine system to initiate the secretion of hormones. These hormones, primarily adrenalin (epinephrine) and cortisol, flood the bloodstream and travel throughout the body to deliver information to cells and systems that will aid in creating the ability to be more speedy and powerful.

We do not need (or want) parasympathetic response systems to operate at high capacity when trying to escape from a lion. Their work is therefore suppressed in order to divert energy to those vital systems involved in increasing speed and power. For example, you do not need the immune system or your reproductive system to help you escape from the lion.

### What does the fight or flight response look like in the moment?

In the moment of feeling threatened, immediate and significant changes occur in our bodies, including: increased heart rate, blood pressure and respiration; the heart-lung system gets to work pumping more blood to the muscles and supplying more oxygen to the muscles.

Also, increased blood sugar allows for rapid energy and accelerated metabolism to facilitate emergency action. Blood thickens to increase oxygen supply (red cells), to enable better defense from infections (white cells) and to stop bleeding quickly (platelets). Senses sharpen, pupils dilate; hearing improves, etc. all in an effort to increase responsiveness.

The body prioritizes blood flow. There is increased blood supply to peripheral muscles, heart, and the brain regions involved in basic/motor functions; whereas blood supply is decreased to the digestive system and irrelevant brain regions, such as speech areas (which is why it's hard to find our words in a crisis). This also causes secretion of body wastes, leaving the body lighter.

Additionally, heightened secretion of adrenaline and other stress hormones further increases response and strengthens relevant systems. Secretion of endorphins (nature's painkillers) is also increased, providing an instant defense against pain. There are even more systems involved in the fight or flight response and even more consequences to it but I think you get the picture.

It is clear the fight or flight response is crucial to dealing with short-term dangers. However it should be equally clear how bad it is for dealing with long-term stress. Just keep in mind the fact that, while all that stimulation is going on enabling us to address the emergency, the immune system is being suppressed. We can see how a suppressed immune system may be helpful in the short run but it's a very poor long term solution... to any problem. Yet people who live with chronic stress (people who constantly perceive danger or attack) are continually activating their fight or flight response. *Which means they are also perpetually suppressing their immune system!* The grave consequences of long-term stress on our body and mind are a direct result of this suppression, and the over activation of adrenalin systems often leads to adrenal fatigue and chronic illness.

Adrenaline is by far the most important single hormone regarding stress - taking a major role in the stress reaction. Adrenaline in the right amounts at the right times is necessary to our survival. However, too much Adrenaline is like a huge oil-spill to the ecology of the body. Exacting a steep price and taking a lot more time and resources to clear it out than it does to launch it.

## Stress and the Adrenal Glands

Unlike our ancestors, we live with constant stress. Instead of occasional, acute demands followed by rest, we're constantly overworked, undernourished, exposed to environmental toxins, worrying about others — with no let-up.

Every challenge to the mind and body creates a demand on the adrenal glands. And the list of challenges is endless: lack of sleep, a demanding boss, the threat of losing your job, financial pressures, personality conflicts, yo-yo dieting, relationship turmoil, death or illness of loved ones, skipping meals, reliance on stimulants like caffeine or carbs, digestive problems, over-exercise, illness or infection, unresolved emotional issues from our past or present, fear of the future and on and on. The result is adrenal glands that are constantly on high alert. And when the adrenal glands get going, one of the first things they do is secrete cortisol.

## The Destructive Effect of High Cortisol Levels

What is cortisol? In its normal function, cortisol helps us meet the demands and challenges of emergency response by converting proteins into energy, releasing glycogen and counteracting inflammation. It's powerful stuff. For a short time, that's okay. But at sustained high levels, cortisol gradually tears your body down.

Sustained high cortisol levels will:

- destroy healthy muscle and bone
- slow down healing and normal cell regeneration
- co-opt biochemicals needed to make other vital hormones
- impair digestion, metabolism and mental function
- interfere with healthy endocrine function; and
- weaken your immune system.

Sustain it too long and it becomes Adrenal Fatigue. Adrenal Fatigue may be a factor in many conditions, including fibromyalgia, hypothyroidism, chronic fatigue syndrome, arthritis, and more. It can also be associated with a host of unpleasant signs and symptoms, from acne to hair loss.

## What is Adrenal Fatigue in Men [42]

**NOTE:** In Appendix D you will find Dr. Wilson's Adrenal Fatigue Questionnaire from *Adrenal Fatigue: The 21st Century Stress Syndrome* by Dr. James L. Wilson. You may want to take this test to see how you are doing physically.

Male Adrenal Fatigue occurs when a man's adrenal glands cannot adequately meet the demands of stress. The adrenal glands mobilize the body's responses to every kind of stress (whether it's physical, emotional, or psychological) through hormones that regulate energy production, immune function, heart rate, muscle tone and basically everything that enables you to cope with stress. Prolonged stress can cause your adrenals to become over stimulated, particularly in the production of cortisol, thus causing them to become fatigued. During adrenal fatigue your adrenal glands still function, but not well enough to maintain optimal levels of cortisol. Most adrenal fatigue in men is the result of daily stress.

Other factors can make you even more susceptible to male adrenal fatigue, such as poor diet, substance abuse, too little sleep or rest, chronic illness and hormone imbalances just to name a few.

### Facts About Male Adrenal Failure

*Fact:* Over-stimulation of your adrenals can be caused either by a very intense single stress, or by chronic or repeated stresses that have a cumulative effect.

*Fact:* Between 50-80% of men experience some form of adrenal fatigue due to stress or stress-related problems.

*Fact:* Cortisol plays a pivotal role hormone balance. For example, thyroid function in the body depends on balanced levels of cortisol.

### Symptoms of Adrenal Fatigue in Men

If you are a man exhibiting any of the following symptoms, it is possible you are experiencing adrenal fatigue:

- You feel tired for no reason.
- You have trouble getting up in the morning, even when you go to bed at a reasonable hour.
- You are feeling rundown or overwhelmed.
- You have difficulty bouncing back from stress or illness.
- You crave salty and sweet snacks.
- You feel more awake, alert and energetic after 6PM than you do all day.

### Adrenal Fatigue Treatment for Men

Adrenal fatigue can wreak havoc in a man's life. It can take time to clear up as well. With each increment of reduction in adrenal function, every organ and system in your body is more profoundly affected. As adrenal fatigue worsens, changes occur in your metabolism, fluid and electrolyte balance, heart and cardiovascular system and even your sex drive. Many other alterations take place at the biochemical and cellular levels in response to adrenal fatigue and compensate for the decrease in adrenal hormones cortisol and DHEA. Your body does its best to make up for under-functioning adrenal glands, but it does so at a price. The price is hormone imbalance and all its consequences.

REVIEW YOUR TEST RESULTS

People with these symptoms can get an adrenal fatigue test, which consists of a series of tests of cortisol levels. And the results — in over thousands of cases — are remarkably consistent: only 10–15% have cortisol levels indicating healthy adrenal function, while 85–90% suffer impaired function, ranging from significant adrenal stress to complete adrenal exhaustion.

The effects of adrenal dysfunction can be profound: fatigue and weakness, suppression of the immune system, muscle and bone loss, moodiness or depression, hormonal imbalance, skin problems, autoimmune disorders and dozens of other symptoms and health concerns

**Natural Adrenal Support — How to Restore Healthy Adrenal Function**

The first step is to have a full physical exam, to be certain there are no serious underlying medical issues causing your symptoms. In my experience, people with mild to moderate adrenal fatigue can see significant improvement through these simple steps:

- Enrich your nutrition, reduce carbohydrates, and cut back on stimulants.

- Consider nutritional supplements that support adrenal function. Start with a high-quality multivitamin–mineral complex rich in stress vitamins, minerals, and essential fatty acids. To learn more about how certain herbs help restore adrenal balance, talk to an herbalist or naturopath about the best combination of herbs for you.

| Adrenal draining | Adrenal restoring |
| --- | --- |
| - Drinks that contain caffeine | - Ginseng <br> - Eleuthero/Siberian ginseng (in the morning) |

| Adrenal draining | Adrenal restoring |
|---|---|
| • Alcohol | • Herbal teas like chamomile, passionflower, valerian |
| • Gatorade | • Vegetable juice (with salt), like V-8 |

- Reduce stress, include moderate exercise and take more time for yourself. It's helpful to make a list of your stressors, especially those that are ongoing or self-imposed.

- Get more rest. Your body needs time to heal!

- Use a good adrenal supplement to rejuvenate the adrenal glands.

- Learn basic stress control techniques such as deep breathing.

- Ensure that you have healthy balanced hormones: testosterone in men, thyroid in men, DHEA in men, and if possible human growth hormone.

- Be "creatively active."

- Use a "brain food" supplement—the brain is a special muscle – it requires special nutrients.

- Eat a sensible diet.

**Vitamin B5**

Of all the vitamins linked with adrenal fatigue, vitamin B5 stands out as the most important. Dr. James Wilson, author of *"Adrenal Fatigue: The 21st Century Stress Syndrome,"* echoes this view and recommends between 600 and 1,200mg of B5 per day. This vitamin, also known as panthothenic acid, is a precursor for a substance called acetyl co-enzyme A, a vital co-factor for the production of many adrenal hormones. Dr. Wilson explains that taking pantothenic acid rarely results in adverse reactions, unlike some herbs typically suggested for adrenal fatigue.

**Vitamin C**

Experts like Dr. Wilson consider cortisol and DHEA as the two most important hormones secreted by the adrenal cortex. In tests of adrenally fatigued men, both cotisol and DHEA levels are consistently low. Vitamin C supplementation can help restore healthier levels of each; in fact, cortisol production cannot occur at all without sufficient vitamin C. Dr. Rodger Murphree, a board-certified chiropractic physician who has written five books on dealing with difficult medical problems, suggests that men with adrenal fatigue take at least 1,800mg of vitamin C each day. Dr. Murphree uses the bowel tolerance test and, using this method, finds that some men may even require 8,000mg each day.

### Zinc

More an element than a vitamin, zinc is a mineral that plays a major role in the regulation of hormones in the body. This becomes particularly relevant in men suffering from adrenal fatigue since disruptions in cortisol and DHEA can often hinder the production of other hormones such as testosterone. Studies show zinc can protect the body from the negative effects of cortisol, as well as boost testosterone and growth hormone. Zinc, a component of more than 80 enzymes in the body, forms part of Dr. Wilson's daily recommendations for men looking to support their adrenal glands

People with more entrenched symptoms, or those who have reached complete adrenal exhaustion, may need further intervention. Finally, we can never underestimate the power of perceived stress. Guilt, pain from past hurts, self-destructive habits, unresolved relationship problems — your past and present emotional experience may be functioning as an ever-present stressor in your life. Dealing directly with these problems is far more beneficial than spending a lifetime compensating for the stress they create.

In all but the most extreme cases, you can expect to see dramatic improvement in four to six months. For mild to moderate adrenal fatigue, the turnaround can be faster. Remember, you may feel as though you're just too tired to make changes now, but by moving forward in incremental stages you'll build the strength you need to stay with it.

CHAPTER SIX

## *Tying it All Together and Getting Into Solution*

### Getting Into Solution

I hope it has become clear to you at this point that attachment issues are not gender based, and neither is codependency. What does seem to be gender influenced is the way Codependency symptoms are expressed.

This means that healing will not be linear – meaning a simple series of steps from A to B to C to Health. Instead you will be addressing multiple issues simultaneously, which may feel more like a spiral than a straight line.

| Anxious or Avoidant Attachment History | Male Gender Role Beliefs | Anxious or Avoidant Behavior Patterns | Inhabiting Your Body |
|---|---|---|---|

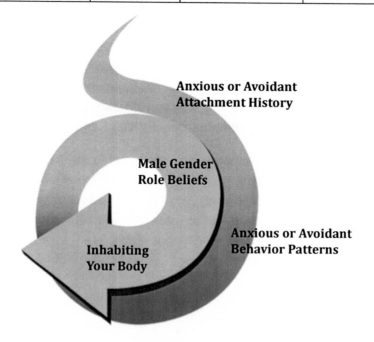

**Anxious or Avoidant Attachment History**

**Male Gender Role Beliefs**

**Anxious or Avoidant Behavior Patterns**

**Inhabiting Your Body**

## How Do I Start????

### Support

Find a guide or support person. Ask for help. This could mean finding a sponsor in Codependent's Anonymous or Al-Anon. It could mean finding a therapist who knows about codependency. It could mean joining a men's group led by a therapist or counselor, or even a men's group like "Nation of Men" where you might find a mentor. *The important thing is to challenge your instinct to "do this yourself" and allow someone to have the answers you do not have.* The first step in any situation is to recognize that you need help if you are going to make substantial and lasting changes in your life. If you could do it this yourself, you would have done it already – we both know that's true.

### Cognitive Life Raft

Learning about Codependency for Males allows you to create a "cognitive life-raft" of understanding. Uncomfortable feelings are less likely to derail me when I see what's happening behind the scenes. Reading this book is an excellent start!

### Review Male Gender Role Quiz

Review your Male Gender Role Conformity test. Some beliefs about "being male" are held so deeply we're not even aware of them. Put words to these beliefs. Think about them. How do these "rules" impact your past and present relationships? You must become familiar with your rules because they pop up again and again as you begin to change your behaviors. You may find your "male rules" are even harder to challenge than your attachment style. Part of Travis Schermer's approach with male clients involves finding models of masculinity.

One surprising model who often comes up is Mr. Rogers. According to Schermer, clients see him not only as masculine but also as a man who was very emotionally aware and present with others. Schermer helps clients identify significant men in their own lives and then delve into what it means for those individuals to be men and how they show their masculinity. This process helps clients recognize qualities they've picked up from others and creates awareness how they in turn impact the lives of others.

For example, a client might come to understand why he believes that "real men" don't talk about their feelings and how that belief is hurting his wife. "It creates this sense of agency," Schermer says. "[Clients say], 'If I knew that this would happen, I would never have let it happen.'" [43]

## Review your Intimacy Questionnaire

Review your Intimacy Questionnaire and become familiar with your attachment style. How did it develop? How have you played out this style in relationships with others (family, friends, co-workers) in the past, and how are you playing out these patterns currently?

*Steven has been meeting with his counselor for the last two months and steadily becoming clearer about his relationship history. As he reflects on it, he can see how he's always been chosen by women, women who tend to be focused, strong-willed and "sure" that he is right for them. While he has always seen himself as "easy going" and flexible, he is also aware that most of his friends have never liked his partners. They have seen the women in Steven's life as bossy, judgmental and controlling. His current girlfriend, who also chose him, tends to be direct and ambitious. She's been complaining about feeling alone in the relationship, frustrated by making all the decisions. She is asking him to "step up his game." Steven admits to his counselor that he is afraid to do this because "she may not like what I have to say," and he may lose yet another relationship. His experience growing up was that disagreement meant the "silent treatment" for the next 2 weeks. Being ignored was so painful that he found being "chosen" as an adult to be reassuring even if it meant losing his voice.*

## Inhabiting Your Own Body

Inhabiting your own body means acknowledging you have physical and emotional feelings. You will have to learn to notice your physical responses when situations are happening (like feeling nauseous) and tune into your physical cues (such as clenched fist, tight neck, stomach clenching) which signal when the situation you're facing is affecting you.

When we have painful or difficult experiences and we're unable to cope with the pain (or just afraid of it), we often dismiss these painful emotions and either get busy, exercise more, drink or eat a bit more or just pretend nothing happened. When we do this we don't feel the emotion, resulting in what's called repressed, suppressed or buried emotions. These feelings stay in our muscles, ligaments, stomach, midriff and auras. These emotions remain buried within us until we bring them back up and feel them, thus releasing them. Burying emotions for the long-term tends to cause physical illness.

Here is a partial list of methods people employ to avoid feeling their emotions:

- Ignoring your feelings
- Pretending something hasn't happened
- Overeating
- Eating foods loaded with sugar and fat
- Excessive drinking of alcohol
- Excessive use of recreational drugs
- Using prescription drugs such as tranquilizers or Prozac
- Exercising compulsively
- Any type of compulsive behavior
- Excessive sex with or without a partner
- Always keeping busy so you can't feel
- Constant intellectualizing and analyzing
- Excessive reading or TV
- Working excessively
- Keeping conversations superficial
- Burying angry emotions under the mask of peace and love

Repressed or buried emotions can cause major difficulties in the physical body and energetic systems. They affect all your relationships, and they especially affect your ability to grow spiritually and be available in your relationships.

Emotions repressed for the long-term can cause serious illness including cancer, arthritis, chronic fatigue, and many other major health problems.

Maintaining repressed emotions in your body creates energy leaks which can lead to fatigue, a sense of vulnerability and low self-confidence.

When you hold repressed emotions, your behavior and reactions to events in the present moment are really reactions to past events. This has a negative effect on all relationships in your life. You cannot be fully present with those you love today until you have released your emotional anchors from the past. You buried emotions because they were too painful and difficult to deal with when they occurred and your reactions to today's events are affected by this pain and hurt that remains buried in your body.

*Kyle has been working with his co-worker Cheryl for the last two years, and has developed tremendous respect for her ability and intelligence. At the same time, Kyle has noticed that Cheryl has a tendency to take credit for his ideas and he is becoming less and less interested in coming to work. He often feels like he is coming down with something, and even went to a movie at lunch the other day. Cheryl is frustrated and is considering asking for a new project partner because she is tired of covering for him. At this point, Kyle is acting out a very old pattern, a pattern where he simply disengages rather than risk confrontation. If Cheryl does get another project partner he will chalk it up to yet another example of how women are disloyal and he always disappoints them.*

It takes a lot of energy to bury emotions and to keep them buried. There isn't much energy left over for other activities when your energy is being used to keep stuffing these emotions back down. By nature, buried emotions want to come up so you can become aware of them, feel them and release them. You work very hard to keep them stuffed down.

**Tips to Inhabit Your Body**

- Be aware of sensations in your body. Emotion always manifests somewhere in the body. Anger might be experienced as a flush of heat in the face, sadness as a tightening of the throat or anxiety as a knot in the stomach. Take a moment to acknowledge the feeling(s). Take a few breaths. Identify these sensations, try to understand what they mean.

- If you are feeling angry, ask yourself what other emotions you might be feeling? Are you really sad underneath, or afraid?

- Learn to put words to what you are feeling. Often it helps to write down or brainstorm ideas before a conversation.

- Identifying and expressing feelings is a learned behavior – and like driving a car, it only takes practice.

- Take the risk of showing your vulnerability with people who feel safe to you. Give yourself permission to be human, it could bring you closer to others and may even bring a sense of relief.

- "Briefly, the best tip I can give a man struggling to express his feelings is to use his cognitive strengths to understand the importance of being emotionally authentic. Learning a vocabulary of feelings is useful. When a man expresses anger (which seems to be the most common and natural emotion he expresses) he can ask himself, 'What would I be feeling if I weren't feeling anger?' Honest answers are usually along the lines of *scared*, *lonely* or *overwhelmed*. That's the first step in actually feeling it."

- Take little steps. Start communicating your emotions to people who love and understand you. Preface it with "This isn't easy for me..." or something similar. Express "a little" emotion. Coleman says: "Start with feelings you can control, find a sympathetic ear and use the term 'a little'." Saying you feel "a little" sad or "a little" scared may be easier.

### Develop an Emotional Vocabulary

Once you begin to recognize these feelings, developing an emotional vocabulary and learning to value the role of emotions can be a guide to healthy relationships with self and others. In the words of Harvard psychologist Daniel Gilbert, Ph.D., "Emotion is a compass that tells us what to do."

Following are several methods you can use to identify what you are really feeling about a person, place, situation or thing. Identifying your emotions is the first step to a rich and healthy emotional life. Use some or all of these methods. Find ones that suit you and let them smooth your journey toward emotional health...

*Morgan will admit that his wife teases him because he has no ability to identify colors, other than his Crayola six-pack! If he's honest he is the same way emotionally. He struggles to identify any emotion beyond sad, mad or glad, both in himself and others. Intellectually he knows feelings are more nuanced, but he's never been very interested in noticing these nuances in himself. He has never seen the point. Recently his relationship with his oldest daughter is becoming increasingly strained. She complains she can't talk with Morgan because he doesn't understand her. He recognizes he's having a hard time empathizing with her and he is very afraid of losing her.*

*Morgan agrees to meet with his daughter's school counselor who may help him learn to "be more emotional." He noticed a poster on the counselor's wall with "feeling faces," and even though he felt slightly ridiculous, he asked her for a paper copy so he could look at it during the week.*

**Listen To Your Thoughts and Daydreams:** We become so accustomed to thinking in certain patterns that we lose awareness of our thoughts and daydreams. Catch those daydreams. Hold the thoughts. Bring them up into your conscious mind. This will reveal a great deal about you. The things you love and hate, and how you see your relationships. If possible, keep a written diary of them for a month or two. Writing down your thoughts and daydreams will help you to organize, experience, and understand your thought patterns. It helps to bring them into a higher level of your awareness. If you keep a written record for a period of time you will begin to see important patterns in your feeling and thinking.

**Identify Your "Little and Unimportant Hurts":** Many people are given to saying "it's not important" or "it doesn't matter" when something is *very* important and reflects a big piece of hurting emotion is buried deep inside. They will describe this hurt as being small and unimportant. Men do this frequently. Write down a detailed description of all the "little and unimportant hurts" that somehow don't go away. Every little hurt you keep remembering that won't go away, regardless of when it happened, must go on this list. Many people have lots of these little hurts from childhood. These emotions are buried within creating difficulties with your health. Identifying these hurts will tell you a great deal about your buried and unexpressed emotions.

*Brian prides himself on having a "long fuse". He has been practicing meditation for quite some time and agrees with Buddhist beliefs about attachments* as a source of suffering. He sees himself as "detached," and others would agree. In fact, they wonder if he actually cares about anything! Brian is the only member of his family who still interacts with his belligerent alcoholic Dad. He knows his father has an illness and "can't help" his behavior. Brain's learned not to take it personally when his dad stands him up for coffee or embarrasses him by flirting with the waitress. Brian's wife notices that after seeing his father Brian tends to be exhausted and emotionally distant. He also sleeps poorly for the next few days. When she brings this to his attention, Brian is puzzled because he has never noticed these changes. He is too busy concentrating on not taking his father's behavior "personally" and moving forward with his week.

**Record What Makes You Feel Strongly For Two Months:** Keep an ongoing record of strong emotions for eight weeks, regardless of the cause. No matter if it's the weather, the traffic, your husband, wife, children, politicians, the stock market, your fellow church members, whatever and whoever it is, simply add it to your list. Try to identify what *really* made you angry. Sadness is a mask for anger, and anger is a mask for fear. If you can identify your real fears (what you are afraid of losing or not having) you are well on your way to emotional health. Again, writing this down will help you see things much more clearly. It will increase your awareness and help you to know your emotional self at a much deeper level.

**Memories That Won't Go Away:** If you keep remembering situations, hurts that happened some time ago, you are guaranteed to have repressed emotions around this person or situation. You will need to pull this situation out and re-feel the hurt around it. Try to document these carefully since these are more than likely causing you actual physical distress. Forgiveness is something that occurs as a result of owning and releasing your emotions. We often reach for forgiveness without doing the work required to release emotions of hurt and anger. Forgiveness is a result of an emotional process. There are no short cuts.

Much of forgiveness takes place when you accept your own humanness and forgive yourself for the decisions you have made in your relationships. This will allow you to extend compassion to yourself, which makes it easier to extend compassion to others who have hurt you as a result of THEIR humanness. Seeing each other from a place of fallibility allows us to extend to each other some grace, to suspend our judgment.

*Eddie has always been afraid of his anger. His childhood was violent with his abusive father and he knows he has a reactive nature. He is particularly careful to monitor himself around his violent father, fearing that if he let himself get "out of control" he would hurt his father badly. Managing his anger is easier now that he is sober. Having started his Fourth Step, he is beginning to recognize just how many resentments he has been carrying toward both of his parents. Toward his father for the violence and toward his mother for allowing it and not leaving or protecting him or his sisters. Eddie is surprised to find his throat tightening. He fights back the tears as he writes down incidents. He is beginning to see ways in which he has intimidated his own son. He is starting to get it when men talk at the meetings about forgiving themselves as part of their eighth and ninth steps.*

**Be Specific About The Emotions You Are Experiencing:** People can get confused when trying to identify their emotions because they speak in general terms rather than specific emotions. A good example of this is depression. You may be experiencing loneliness for people, loneliness for God (spiritual loneliness), boredom and a lack of creativity in your life. You may be feeling abandoned because of a death or divorce. If you just say you're depressed you will have great difficulty releasing the emotion or finding a solution to the situation causing it.

*Now that Eddie is connecting his childhood with his own parenting he is aware that he is having trouble sleeping, his neck is tight, and his chest feels tight. Concerned that he is developing the heart condition which runs in his family, he makes a medical appointment. "I'm not going to get sober just too die" he tells his sponsor. When his heart tests out well, the doctor refers Eddie to a therapist. He finds this confusing since he has never thought about a connection between his feelings and his health. Fortunately recovery has at least taught him to take direction so he makes an appointment. When the therapist asks him about his concerns, Eddie is at a loss because he has spent so much time focusing and controlling his anger that he has no idea what his other feelings might be! The therapist recommends that he spend time jotting down his physical symptoms when they appear and paying attention to his thoughts when the physical pain happens. Then try to guess what someone who is having those thoughts might be feeling. He brings the journal into his sessions for the two of them to explore.*

**Are You Using Sex To Release Your Emotions?** Sex is a normal and healthy part of life. Many people engage in sexual acts (with others, alone, or using Internet pornography) to release emotions buried within them that they have been unable to feel and release. These individuals tend to have a very high sex drive since this is their primary way of releasing pent up emotions. These are people who enjoy sex more than once a day. They appear to be very cerebral or intellectual. Actually, they are highly emotional but very much out of touch with their emotions. If you identify with this description, keep a record of your thoughts/ experiences/fears just prior to engaging in this type of sex. Sex can be used to stuff feelings down so you won't feel them. Identifying those feelings and releasing them will help you move into a much healthier and enjoyable sex life.

**Eating, Drinking, Exercising, or Any Type of Compulsive/Excessive Behavior:** We often go for weeks, even years acting in a manner that feels perfect-ly normal for us. Then we find ourselves overeating, working excessively, drinking daily, engaging in compulsive sex and/or many other types of com-pulsive behavior. We use excessive behavior to stuff our emotions down, ensuring we do not feel them in the moment. We do this because the feel-ings are too painful or we are just too afraid of these feelings and where they might lead us in our thinking and actions.

Try to identify the times when your excessive behavior was triggered, then try to identify the emotion that is causing this behavior as soon as you can. It can be stress or fear of a new job, the death of a friend or partner, difficul-ties with lovers or children. Document these emotions as best as you can. We never do anything without getting something from it. **There is a reason why you are engaged in excessive or compulsive behavior.**

*Andrew is the only son of divorced parents, and has been managing his own time since he was 9 years old. When he was 11, while looking for toilet paper he found a Playboy magazine shoved back in his father's bathroom cabinet. Curious, he started looking at the pictures and found himself in-creasingly aroused. Embarrassed and vaguely aware that he might get in trouble if he said anything, Andrew replaced the magazine and went back outside to play basketball with his neighbor. But he couldn't stop thinking about it, and the next weekend he took the first opportunity to look at the magazine. Unfortunately, he chose to look for the magazine after a terrible fight with his Vicodin-addicted father and he was feeling pretty upset.*

*As he looked at the magazine, Andrew found he wasn't thinking about the fight with his dad anymore. In fact, all he was thinking about were the girls in the pictures and learning to masturbate like they described in the magazine. Andrew is 23 now and has "graduated" to computer porn and Craig's list "hookups." If he doesn't go online he begins to feel anxious and out-of-sorts. It sems the only time he feels calm is when he is acting out sexually. Pornography has become Andrew's only way to self-soothe and also to "feel something."*

**When What You Say and Do Is Not In Sync With What You Feel:** Men go through many situations telling themselves that "it doesn't really matter" or "it's not important enough to argue about." Basically they are buying peace by agreeing to something that deep down they do not agree with. They find themselves feeling unhappy, disgruntled and angry with the individual involved. This type of situation creates tension and unhappiness in relationships. Buying peace at any price creates negative feelings within you.

Identify those situations where you have created depressing feelings within yourself by agreeing to something with which you don't really agree. Write them down. This will be difficult for people who have difficulty saying no, or who are too anxious to please others. But the feelings generated by these situations are very important when dealing with your emotional life. Many times we need to simply excuse things and overlook them. That's normal. But sometimes we do this in situations that affect us deeply. These are the situations we must identify.

*Sam and his wife Shoshanna are aware that he's not much fun to be around during the holidays. In fact, he always dreads them and frustrates his wife every year because he is grumpy when she buys Hanukkah presents he has to pay for. If he was asked, Sam isn't completely sure why he dreads the holidays, but he knows they've been a downer for most of his life. He might tell* you holidays are "too commercial" and "don't mean anything anymore." The part he dreads the most is the Hanukkah dinner, because Shoshanna insists on inviting Sam's parents even though they are not religious people. In fact, his parents tend to arrive late, give the children a $20.00 bill and pat their heads, and rarely stay much past desert. It is clear they are there out of "obligation" and Sam finds himself angry, depressed, anxious and resentful. While Shoshanna knows this is the pattern, she insists on inviting them because "the children deserve to know their grandparents."

Actually, the children don't know their grandparents, because they never interact with them unless it's a holiday. In fact, Sam's parents treated Sam and his sister the same way, and if he gave it some thought he would have to admit watching his parents treat his own children this way brings that childhood back. The truth is Sam would like to exclude his parents next year, but he's too afraid of the conflict with Shoshanna to push the issue. Instead he is grumpy and hard to live with.

**Positive Emotions:**  It is crucial that you identify your positive emotions during these exercises. You are probably very loving, caring, compassionate, trusting, forgiving and generous many times each day. Be certain to include the wonderful and good things about yourself as you identify your emotional self. This provides a realistic picture. If you record only negative emotions, your picture of yourself will be quite distorted. We are all born with a complete range of emotions and each emotion needs to be seen in its full and loving energy.

**The Gentle Whispers of Your Soul:**  Find a quiet place and time to listen to your inner voice of intuition. Everyone has it. Listen with your heart rather than your head. Your heart hears different things than your head does.

There is a very special time just as you are waking up in the morning but before you are fully awake. This is the zone when you can often hear your sub-conscious speaking to you. Listen to your thoughts at this time carefully and you will pick up important messages. Messages that can help you identify your emotions, even your core issues.

One morning about a month before Hanukkah, Sam wakes up earlier than usual. He gets up to make some coffee and sees his daughter has fallen asleep on the couch while studying for an exam later today. Sam feels over-whelming love for her in that moment, and in that same moment remem-bers doing the same thing. Only in his case, he was trying to win parental attention, which was fleeting. As he looks at her sweet face it hits him that his parents don't love his children, and it is possible that his children don't look forward to seeing them because they can feel this disconnection. Es-pecially in contrast to his wife's parents who adore them and can't spend enough time with them!

Sam makes a decision to listen to himself, for once, and tell Shoshanna that he does not want to include his parents. They never ask about it anyway, and usually only agree to come at the last minute. This year, Sam wants to spend the holiday with people who love each other and aren't pretending. As he has this thought, he feels his chest lighten and a smile comes over his face.

**Crying About Your Experience:** Crying is a normal release function for ev-ery human being. We are born with this ability because crying let's us re-lease pain, hurt and the associated stress. Crying (or writing and crying) about what has happened to you can help sort out your experience and understand it. Understanding is crucial for many people. If you've had a very painful experience, write one sentence and sit with this sentence and cry. Then write another sentence and sit and cry. In time, this process will relieve some of the sensitive pain around your experience and eventually make it endurable. With time, the pain around the situation will lesson, as long as you allow yourself to feel it.

I recognize this suggestion is greatly at odds with "male gender role rules," yet crying serves as a pressure relief valve and can create space for the good feelings that follow after a good cleansing. It's worth the potential embarrassment or momentary feeling of weakness to experience the relief that joining the rest of the human race can bring. Other cultures are far more open for men to express the larger range of emotions available to them. Maybe you can channel your inner Italian or Greek to access ALL of you!

**Writing About Your Emotions:** We can play all sorts of games with our minds, denying reality is something we all do. However, it's much harder to do that when we write things down. You don't have to show your list to anyone, but for complete emotional health you have to fully accept your emotions. This acceptance will be accelerated if you write your list and share this list of emotions with one other human being. But be very careful and choose someone who will guarantee you confidentiality. I highly recommend a counselor, minister, psychiatrist or someone trained in this type of work; someone who guarantees confidentiality. A professional can often help you put a healthy perspective on these emotions. Writing this list is important and healing.

The Twelve Step programs have long identified writing as a key tool of recovery. Writing can often help us clarify our thoughts, and we can begin to see themes in our thoughts over time. Writing engages our frontal lobe in a conversation with our limbic system – or emotions – that can help us harness both recognition and eventually problem-solving. Some people find writing calming – it is a relief to stop carrying so many thoughts in your head. Sometimes it helps to write before you sleep for this same reason.

**How To Release Emotions**

Don't be afraid of your emotions. Don't fight them. Don't run away from them. Don't block them out. Welcome your emotions! Be with them, regardless of what they are. We are born with all our emotions. They are neither good nor bad, they just are. There is no need to judge them. Emotions slowly dissipate and disappear if you are willing to feel them and be present with them. Just close your eyes and experience them as deeply as you can.

**Deciding How To Respond To Your Emotions:** Once you have identified a certain emotion you will at times need to decide how to proceed in dealing with it. There are many options that need to be considered carefully. Certain approaches can have very serious effects. You could lose your job, or you could lose your marriage. It's very important to consider your options carefully before saying or doing something that cannot be taken back.

*Rojan has been impulsive his whole life. He would describe himself as passionate and decisive, which is also true about him. However, he is frequently dealing with the consequences of his impulsive decisions, and sometimes* the wreckage includes inconveniencing or hurting others. When this happens, Rojan usually feels guilty and beats up on himself. Upon reviewing his journal writings he notices a theme of distrust; in situation after situation he seems to "take over" decision making because he does not trust the input or competence of others. He cannot bear "waiting" for further consultation, his anxiety builds and all too quickly reaches a point where he has to do something – anything – and tends to pull the trigger prematurely.

As he writes he realizes he fears being blocked or held back. His parent's ongoing fears blocked him and held him back throughout his childhood. Both parents were immigrants and saw America as a violent, unsafe place. They were always reminding him to be careful. While America was a land of opportunity, it was also "scary." He wonders if he has been living his whole life in reaction to his parents instead of being "free" like he has been telling himself.

Following are questions to consider when deciding what response would best suit a particular situation. Remember: Each emotion and situation is different.

* Am I reacting to just this situation or is some past situation involved as well?

* Am I able to discuss the current issue without venting anger?

* Am I able to speak with this person without venting anger?

* Will I be able to talk about how I feel to the person?

* Is a direct approach the best way to proceed?

* What are the consequences of dealing directly with this person/ situation?

* What do I expect from this discussion?

* Are my expectations realistic?

* Should I discuss this with someone else before doing anything?

By asking these questions you will be deciding whether a direct approach is the best approach and if you are ready do this at the present time. If your anger is at a "rage" stage, you need to release some of this anger before attempting to discuss this with anyone.

- **The Physical Part of Releasing Your Emotions:** There are a number of ways you can begin to release your emotions, especially those relating to anger and hurt.

    1. Go into an empty room, or go for a drive alone, and scream, scream as loudly as you can. Scream the words "I hate" or whatever it is you are feeling. So many people have never screamed out their hurt, their rage. Continue to do this as long as it feels right inside. Cry, allow yourself to cry your feeling.

    2. If you cannot scream aloud, imagine you are screaming your rage, hurt, and pain. Imagine it and imagine it. See it, and hear it, and especially, feel it as deeply as you can.

    3. If you are a physical person, take a pillow and keep hitting a chair, your bed, something, feeling your hurt every time you hit that object with the pillow. Every time you hit that pillow say the words "I hate" or "I am frustrated" or whatever it is that you are feeling.

    4. Get yourself a punching bag and hang it in your basement. Then take time to keep hitting that punching bag, releasing your rage.

    5. Take your fists and keep pounding a table saying, "I hate" and just keep doing it.

    6. If you like to write, write about your anger; write about your hate; write about how hurt you are; write about how afraid you really are. Journal about what happened and how it is affecting you today. Write about what you have lost, or what you have never had that has hurt you so deeply. **Feel the feeling! Don't be afraid of it!**

Underneath all the anger, rage, hate and hurt is one basic emotion –
FEAR!

Whatever method you choose it is essential to realize you are currently hating. You are full of rage and anger. The safest way to begin accepting your hate and anger is to *own* your hate and anger. We become so afraid of losing control due to the intensity of our rage, that we run away from it and ignore it. The more you ignore it, the bigger it gets.

One of the most effective techniques for releasing an emotion is concentrating on the emotion rather than what caused it. Forget about what was done or who did it. Concentrate on the "I hate" or "I am angry" or "I am so hurt." It's the emotion you need to release. Don't be afraid to feel your feelings... and feeling them means owning them!

*As Rojan became more aware of his reactivity and its connection to his childhood, he began to notice the anxiety he feels before making an impulsive decision. He could see how his anxiety was a mirror of his parent's anxiety, and how much of his behavior over time was designed to distance himself from this idea. Rather than basing his reactivity in courage, he based it in fear. It just looks differently on the surface. He could feel his anxiety increasing as he focused on this awareness, but he decided to keep writing rather than get a drink or go buy something like he usually would. This decision was "true" courage.*

**Speaking Your Truth –** To release emotions you need to tell one human being, one time only about the situation that caused the feeling buried within you. You need to explain three things in detail; what happened, your feelings around this experience and how this experience is affecting your life today. So often we hide life's happenings because we are ashamed. Somehow we feel things happen to us because we are "bad people." It's important to tell your complete story in detail to one person. This will help you gain a healthier perspective on the situation. However, if you keep talking about the story repeatedly to different people, thinking about it over and over again, this becomes a resentment (a recurring negative thought). This resentment then becomes another problem rather than part of the solution.

Secrets are shame-based and incidents kept secret or feelings hidden from others will make these feelings deeper and longer lasting. Emotional secrets lead to emotional and mental illness.

*Tony has been resistant to going the men's group his counselor has been recommending. He feels strongly that his business is private, and the last thing he needs is to air his dirty laundry with people who are probably as screwed up as he is. Tony doesn't see how it will help to talk about the way his ex-wife screwed him, and has put a wedge between him and his kids. He has admitted to his counselor that she is the only person he has thought about killing in his whole life. His counselor explains the point of the group is to help him change his thinking patterns and find healthy solutions to manage his relationship with his ex-wife.*

*If Tony does not interrupt his thinking, he will remain stuck in his resentment and rage for years. If Tony were to shift feeling victimized he would have to get honest about his contribution to the failure of his marriage, which includes an affair his wife never learned about. He is deeply ashamed of cheating on his wife, something his father did to his mother, and he swore he would never do. The counselor recommends an exercise to help Tony shift the intensity of his resentment towards his ex-wife.*

- **Transmuting Emotions:** Sit in a comfortable chair, close your eyes, put your head back and relax as best you can. Do the following exercise for 10 deep breaths. While concentrating on your breathing, inhale on the count of six, hold this breath to the count of six, exhale to the count of six, and rest to the count of six, and then begin again. If the count of six is too difficult try a count of four or five. Concentrate fully on your process of breathing. Keep doing this exercise until you feel more relaxed and the noises in your head go away.

  Then slowly look for the emotion, find where it is buried in your body. All repressed emotions rest in your body and at times in the aura as well. Anger rests around your belly button area but it can also be seen as a black thread-like substance all through the body. Sadness sits in the midriff area. Emotions can rest anywhere in your body including the muscles, ligaments and bone joints. Take your time, find your emotion.

  Then take time to really see what this emotion looks like. I had a huge amount of sadness. When I finally found it I saw it had the shape of a large mass of clouds, clouds so dense and thick that you couldn't begin to even dent them. These clouds were a very dark gray color.

Once you have found your emotion and described it to yourself, stay with it, hold it, and be with it. Do not try to do anything to it – VERY IMPORTANT- just be with it. By being with it you begin to integrate this emotion into your very consciousness and this is the next step in releasing your emotion. As you go back to visit your buried emotion week after week you will find the shape getting smaller and smaller until eventually it just disappears. This is what is meant by "transmuting emotions." It takes many months to transmute an emotion in this way, but it's a powerful method for releasing emotions.

**Releasing Resentments:** A resentment is a recurring anger we maintain by repeatedly thinking about something someone has done to us, reliving all the particulars around this situation and reviving the anger, hate, hurt or whatever negative feeling we initially experienced.

Pray for the person you are resenting. Wish for this person every wonderful thing you would want to have in your most perfect life. Wish them blessing and good fortune in all things. In time, this type of a prayer will release you from your resentment. This is difficult.

You can also write about this person. Write all the negative qualities you see in this person. Then write about all the positive qualities you see in this person. Eventually, by writing about the different qualities, a shift will occur within you bringing peace of mind.

You can write about the situation, what the person did to you and how it affected you, how it made you feel. Write about how you reacted to this situation, what you said and what you did. When we accept responsibility for our own behavior the resentment often disappears.

**Shifting Your Perspective:** Life brings injustice, abuse, bad luck and difficult emotions (hurt, anger, self-pity and depression to name a few). It's easy to look at what others have done that you consider wrong, and these wrongs are very real. It's not as easy to look at your response to the real wrong or injustice done to you. Someone might have demeaned and degraded you. Did you punish them in some manner for their behavior? Was your response to the situation a healthy and loving response? Emotions around injustice of any kind are complex. Once we accept personal responsibility for our responses, the emotions around a given situation tend to lose their hold over us. It's important to honor that an injustice has occurred. But it's equally important to be ready to release it from your life, which involves looking at your own behavior and accepting responsibility for your own actions.

*Carlos has just been released after serving a two year stretch for a crime he did not commit. He feels he was racially profiled, denied a decent attorney and he believes with proper representation he would not have served time but rather been placed on probation. He is most likely correct. The reality is Carlos had priors for theft and there is no doubt his history was part of why he was given jail time.*

*As he speaks to his Pastor after his release, he admits he had been committing a string of home break-ins when he was picked up for someone else's commercial building burglary. While it's true his sentence was an injustice because he was wrongly accused, he HAD committed multiple crimes which were never linked to him. If he's honest, he served time he probably deserved. If he's completely honest, his methamphetamine addiction was the real reason behind the thefts.*

**Detach Yourself:** When your emotions are running high and you are having difficulty reducing the intensity, try to detach yourself from the situation and the emotion. Try to imagine the same situation happening to someone else. Try to see if the behavior would be the same if someone else were in your situation. If the answer is yes then you can begin to see the experience is not necessarily being focused at you. The other person is probably acting unconsciously and you just happen to be "in their way." Detaching yourself in this manner can help you move through very difficult situations without taking the abuse personally. You might need to terminate the situation causing the emotions, but your detachment allows you to look at things more rationally and quietly.

*George is heartbroken after he discovers that his wife of 15 years has been sleeping with a co-worker. This is not the first time a woman has betrayed*

*George, and he is filled with bitterness as he ruminates on "all the things I did for her" and her lack of gratitude. From George's vantage point, his compulsive work schedule was necessary to "give her everything she wanted." Besides, he always made it up to her with expensive jewelry, "proof" that he loved her. He protected her from the stress of his work by refusing to talk about work when he was at home, and made sure that he supported every new project she wanted to undertake. "I never stopped her from doing anything she wanted to do."*

*As George outlines various sacrifices he's made for his wife, his sister surprises him by asking, "Did she ever ask you for any of those things?" Then she added, "I wonder if she was lonely in that big house all by herself." Tony's first response was to get aggravated and feel misunderstood, thinking. "Yet another ungrateful woman." However, as the next few days passed, he kept hearing his sister's comments in his head, and began to wonder if there is something about him that makes women cheat on him. This was an incredibly painful thought.*

**Knowing Your Fears:** What fears lay beneath your emotions? You will need to know and understand your fears. To do this you will have to swallow some pride and admit and accept that you have many fears that are affecting what you do each day. These fears are often at the unconscious level. Do you fear loneliness, abandonment, adventure or the unknown? How about losing face or prestige, ridicule, poverty, death or suffering? How scary is going unrecognized for your work and effort; losing your wife or husband? The list is endless.

Fears are tricky things. Sometimes you need to ignore them and just act unafraid. For example, if you're afraid to say no, your fear will leave as you begin to say no when needed. It's like exercising an atrophied muscle. The more you use it the easier it gets. Other fears are a healthy warning that something is very wrong. For example, a person might be afraid of another person. This fear might be the signal to avoid that person, to leave the relationship.

As you become aware of your fears and own them as truly yours, a day will come when you will notice one of them has somehow disappeared. That's the way it is with fear. As you live a life in tune with your emotions, a life focused on coming from a place of love, you will find that many of your fears simply disappear.

**Accepting Responsibility For Your Emotions:** Taking care of ourselves is the way to love ourselves in a wholesome and healthy manner. This means accepting responsibility for our emotions. Remember, emotions are not good or bad. They just are. Don't punish yourself or be too hard on yourself. Balance is the key word. Each human being is very human, and that means each one of us is born with a full range of emotions.

## What About Reversing the Effects of Cortisol and Adrenal Fatigue?

### OXYTOCIN

Oxytocin is a hormone that helps you relax by reducing blood pressure and cortisol levels. It increases pain thresholds, has anti-anxiety effects and stimulates various types of positive social interaction. In addition, it promotes growth and healing. Oxytocin is truly the body's wonder drug.

Check out this interview with Kerstin Uväs-Moberg, M.D., Ph. D, author of *The Oxytocin Factor*. She is a recognized world authority on oxytocin:

http://www.lifesciencefoundation.org/cmoxtyocin.html

Oxytocin, which was first noticed during birth labor and in nursing mothers in 1906, acts as both a hormone and a neuropeptide. It triggers a complex series of reactions that enhance your body's relaxation and calmness. This is important for two reasons. The first is the immediate health benefit of lowering stress-related symptoms and the second is how repeated dosages of oxytocin seem to convert this immediate benefit into a long-lasting effect. In clinical trials on animals, those who received as little as one dose per day for 5 days needed little additional oxytocin to stay calm for up to 3 weeks.[43] This suggests oxytocin can offer stressed human beings a way to open up new pathways, to help them relax and restore calm both immediately and over the long term.

Oxytocin does two key things: (1) lowers blood pressure and other stress-related responses, and (2) increases positive social behaviors, such as friendliness and desire to connect. Oxytocin is a hormone released into the bloodstream by nerve centers inside the brain, making it available to the entire body on short notice.

Oxytocin release can be triggered by various types of sensory stimulation, such as touch, smell or sight. Certain foods may trigger oxytocin release as well. But perhaps most significantly for our purposes, some purely psychological mechanisms can trigger the release of oxytocin. This means positive interaction involving touch and psychological support may be health-promoting. The social interaction of daily life (as well as a positive environment) continuously activate this system.[105] In addition, various types of psychotherapy delivering support, warmth and empathy are likely to induce similar effects, thus enhancing the positive impact of these therapies

## Stimulants that Cause the Brain to Release Oxytocin

**Sexual intercourse**: Oxytocin is released during orgasm which accounts for that warm afterglow we experience. Orgasm increases oxytocin in the body to twice its normal level.

**Eating comfort foods**: Eating your favorite food such as chocolate, ice-cream or any meal that you really enjoy will release oxytocin.

**Being kind to others**: That good feeling you get after saying or doing something nice for another person is also due to the release of oxytocin.

**Making physical contact with others**: Hugs, cuddles, kissing and touching all can initiate a release of oxytocin.

**Massage**: Oxytocin is released during muscle relaxation and touch.

**Surrounding yourself with great friend's**: Camaraderie and closeness to those we value and care about increases oxytocin. Time spent with hostile or negative people decreases oxytocin.

**Meditation**: Meditating daily for 20 minutes increases oxytocin.

**Acupuncture**: This eastern medical practice is proven to increase oxytocin levels which explains why it may be such an effective treatment for some people.

**Pets**: Having affection for a pet releases oxytocin. Caring for and stroking an animal's fur releases oxytocin.

**Sensory experiences**: Comforting sights, sounds and smells can boost oxytocin levels. The smell of foods you enjoyed while growing up, the sounds of the ocean waves or even certain lighting can be effective. When senses have a positive emotional connection they tend to trigger oxytocin release.

**Activity**: Walking, swimming in warm water and physical exercise work well to boost oxytocin levels, says Kerstin Uvas-Moberg, PhD.

**Deep interaction**: Intimate eye contact and "deep interaction" are also advised by Dr. Uvas-Mosberg.

Having oxytocin in the blood has a calming effect on the body.[106] It has been used in scientific studies to reduce withdrawal effects experienced by rats from being addicted to heroin, morphine, cocaine and methamphetamine. It reduces appetite cravings which leads to weight loss. It's the body's natural antidepressant and anti-anxiety hormone.

Heres the thing about oxytocin: The more you give, the more you get! Oxytocin profoundly effects you feel and how you view the world. Connecting with others, being kind and nurturing, these are the keys to feeling wonderful.

# *End Notes*

1.  Crocker Cook, Mary. (2011) Awakening Hope. A Developmental, Behavioral, Biological Approach to Codependency Treatment. Robertson Publishing

2.  Feeney, J.A., & Noller, P. (1996). *Adult Attachment.* London: Sage pg. 122

3.  Gregor (1985). Anxious Pleasures. University of Chicago Press.

4.  Hardy, M. Hough, J. (1991) Against the Wall. Men's Reality in a Codependent Culture. A Hazelden Book. Ballentine books, New York. Pg 4

5.  Levant, R. (1992). Toward the reconstruction of masculinity. Journal of Family Psychology, 5, 379–402.

6.  Levant et al (1992). The male role: An investigation of norms and stereotypes. Journal of Mental Health Counseling, 14, 325-337.

7.  John Donnelly, LAADC conversation over dinner in Sacramento, CA 2013.

8.  Hardy, M. Hough, J. (1991) Against the Wall. Men's Reality in a Codependent Culture. A Hazelden Book. Ballentine books, New York. Pg 88

9.  Ibid, pg. 8

10. David & Brannon (1976). The Forty-nine percent majority: The male sex role. Addison-Wesley.

11. Hardy, M. Hough, J. (1991) Against the Wall. Men's Reality in a Codependent Culture. A Hazelden Book. Ballentine books, New York. Pg 94

12. Ibid. pg 52

13. Ibid. pg. 4

14. O'Neil, J. M. (2008). Summarizing 25 years of research on men's gender role conflict using the Gender Role Conflict Scale: New

research paradigms and clinical implications. The Counseling Psychologist, 36, 358.

15. Ibid. 353

16. Bergman, S.J. (1995). Men's psychological development: A relational perspective In R.F. Levant & W.S Pollack (Eds.), A new psychology of men (pp. 33-67). New York: Basic Books.

17. Bergman, Stephen J, MD, PhD, Male Relational Dread, Psychiatric Annals 26. 1 (Jan 1996): 24-28.

18. Griffin, D. & Dauer, R. (2012) Addiction Magazine. Rethinking Men and Codependency.

19. Ibid.

20. Jordan, J. V. (1997). Relational development: Therapeutic implications of empathy and shame. In J. V. Jordan (Ed.), *Women's growth in diversity* (pp. 138–161). New York: Guilford Press.

21. Hartling, L. M., Rosen, W., Walker, M., & Jordan, J. V. (2000). *Shame and humiliation: From isolation to relational transformation* (Work in Progress No. 88). Wellesley, MA: Stone Center Working Paper Series.

22. Eisler, R.M., & Skidmore, J.R. (1987). Masculine gender role stress: Scale development and component factors in the appraisal of stressful situations. Behavior Modification, 11, 123-136.

23. Eisler, R.M. (1995). The relationship between masculine gender role stress and men's health risk: The validation of the construct. In R.F. Levant & W.S. Pollack (Eds.), A new psychology of men (pp. 207-225). New York: Basic Books.

24. Eisler, R.M., Skidmore, J.R., & Ward, C.H. (1988). Masculine gender stress: Predictor of anger, anxiety, and health-risk behaviors. Journal of Personality Assessment, 52, 133-141.

25. Watkins, P.L., Eisler, R.M., Carpenter, L., Schechtman, K.B., & Fisher, E.B. (1991). Psychosocial and physiological correlates of male gender role stress among employed adults. Behavioral Medicine, 17, 86-90

26. Ibid.

27. Baffi, C.R., Redican, K.J., Sefchick, M.K., & Impara, J.C. (1991). Gender role identity, gender role stress, and health behaviors: An exploratory study of selected college males. *Health Values, 15,* 9-18

28. Eisler, R.M. (1995). The relationship between Masculine Gender Role Stress and men's health risk: The validation of a construct. In R.F. Levant & W.S. Pollack (Eds.), *A new psychology of men* (pp. 207-225). New York: Basic Books.

29. Eisler, R.M., Skidmore, J.R., & Ward, C.H. (1988). Masculine gender-role stress: Predictor of anger, anxiety, and health-risk behavior. *Journal of Personality Assessment, 52,* 133-141..

30. Lash, S.J., Eisler, R.M., & Schulman, R.S. (1990). Cardiovascular reactivity to stress in men: Effects of masculine gender role stress appraisal and masculine performance challenge. *Behavior Modification, 14,* 3-20.

31. Fragoso, J.M., & Kashubeck, S. (2000). Machismo, gender role conflict, and mental health in Mexican American men. Psychology of Men & Masculinity, 2, 87-97.

32. Good, G.E., Robertson, J.M., O'Neil, J., Fitzgerald, L.F., Stevens, M., DeBord, K.A., et al. (1995). Male gender role conflict: Psychometric issues and relations to psychological stress. Journal of Counseling Psychology, 42, 3-10.

33. Sharpe, M.J., & Heppner, P.P. (1991). Gender role, gender role conflict, and psychological well-being in men. Journal of Counseling Psychology, 38, 323-330.

34. Blazina, C., & Watkins, C.E., Jr. (1996). Masculine gender role conflict: Effects on college men's psychological well-being, chemical substance use, and attitudes toward help-seeking. Journal of Counseling Psychology, 43, 461-465.

35. Cournoyer, R.J., & Mahalik, J.R. (1995). Cross-sectional study of gender role conflict examining college-aged and middle-aged men. Journal of Counseling Psychology, 42, 11-19.

36.  Rando, R.A., Rogers, J.R., & Brittan-Powell, C.S. (1998). Gender role onflict and college men's sexually aggressive attitudes and behavior. Journal of Mental Health Counseling, 20, 359-369

37.  Eisler, R.M., Skidmore, J.R., & Ward, C.H. (1988). Masculine gender stress: Predictor of anger, anxiety, and health-risk behaviors. Journal of Personality Assessment, 52, 133-141.

38.  Watkins, P.L., Eisler, R.M., Carpenter, L., Schechtman, K.B., & Fisher, E.B. (1991). Psychosocial and physiological correlates of male gender role stress among employed adults. Behavioral Medicine, 17, 86-90

39.  Kidd, M. (2002). Suicide and manhood. Manhood online. Retrieved October 18, 2002, from: http://www.manhood.com.au/scripts/manhood

40.  Connell, R.W. (1996). Masculinities. Sydney: Allen & Unwin.

41.  Hassan, R. (1995). Suicide explained: The Australian experience. Melbourne: Melbourne University Press.

42.  What is Adrenal fatigue in Men? http://www.renewman.com/male-hormones/adrenal-fatigue

43.  Travis Schermer: http://ct.counseling.org/2010/08/men-welcome-here/

44.  Dr. Kerstin Uvas-Moberg. http://www.lifesciencefoundation.org/cmoxytocin.html

# Appendix  A

## *Attachment Style Quiz*

### What is Your Attachment Style? Here's a Quiz

To prepare for the following discussion on the developmental origins of codependency, I have included this questionnaire. Today's attachment researchers find it helpful to look at the proportion of anxiety and avoidance that we may experience in relation to emotional intimacy. Allow yourself about twenty minutes in total and grab a calculator because scoring is a bit complicated. In fact, if you are in emotional pain, you may just want to review the questions to "get the gist" of where I am going in this section. Enjoy your internal exploration.

### The Experiences in Close Relationships-Revised (ECR-R) Questionnaire
### Fraley, Waller, and Brennan (2000)

The statements below concern how you feel in emotionally intimate relationships. Answer the questions in terms of how you *generally* experience relationships, not just in what is happening in a current relationship. Respond to each statement by giving a number from 1 through 7 to indicate how much you agree or disagree with the statement. 1 = strongly disagree and 7 = strongly agree. At the end of the survey, you will find some slightly complicated scoring instructions. Trust me. You can get through this. Use a calculator. Or, again, you can bag scoring the test at all!

1. strongly disagree
2. disagree
3. disagree somewhat
4. neutral
5. agree somewhat
6. agree
7. strongly agree

1. It's not difficult for me to get close to my partner.

2. I often worry that my partner will not want to stay with me.

3. I often worry that my partner doesn't really love me.

4. It helps to turn to my romantic partner in times of need.

5. I often wish that my partner's feelings for me were as strong as my feelings for him or her.

6. I worry a lot about my relationships.

7. I feel comfortable depending on romantic partners.

8. When I show my feelings for romantic partners, I'm afraid they will not feel the same about me.

9. I rarely worry about my partner leaving me.

10. My partner only seems to notice me when I'm angry.

11. I feel comfortable depending on romantic partners.

12. I do not often worry about being abandoned.

13. My romantic partner makes me doubt myself.

14. I find that my partner(s) don't want to get as close as I would like.

15. I'm afraid that I will lose my partner's love.

16. My desire to be very close sometimes scares people away.

17. I worry that I won't measure up to other people.

18. I find it easy to depend on romantic partners.

19. I prefer not to show a partner how I feel deep down.

20. I feel comfortable sharing my private thoughts and feelings with my partner.

21. I worry that romantic partners won't care about me as much as I care about them.

22. I find it difficult to allow myself to depend on romantic partners.

23. I'm afraid that once a romantic partner gets to know me, he or she won't like who I really am.

24. I am very comfortable being close to romantic partners.

25. I don't feel comfortable opening up to romantic partners.

26. I prefer not to be too close to romantic partners.

27. I get uncomfortable when a romantic partner wants to be very close.

28. I find it relatively easy to get close to my partner.

29. I usually discuss my problems and concerns with my partner.

30. I tell my partner just about everything.

31. Sometimes romantic partners change their feelings about me for no apparent reason.

32. When my partner is out of sight, I worry that he or she might become interested in someone else.

33. I am nervous when partners get too close to me.

34. It's easy for me to be affectionate with my partner.

35. It makes me mad that I don't get the affection and support I need from my partner.

36. My partner really understands me and my needs.

## Score Key

| | 1 Strongly disagree | 2 Disagree | 3 Disagree somewhat | 4 Neutral | 5 Agree somewhat | 6 Agree | 7 Strongly agree |
|---|---|---|---|---|---|---|---|
| 1 | (7) | (6) | (5) | (4) | (3) | (2) | (1) |
| 2 | | | | | | | |
| 3 | | | | | | | |
| 4 | (7) | (6) | (5) | (4) | (3) | (2) | (1) |
| 5 | | | | | | | |
| 6 | | | | | | | |
| 7 | (7) | (6) | (5) | (4) | (3) | (2) | (1) |
| 8 | | | | | | | |
| 9 | (7) | (6) | (5) | (4) | (3) | (2) | (1) |
| 10 | | | | | | | |
| 11 | (7) | (6) | (5) | (4) | (3) | (2) | (1) |
| 12 | (7) | (6) | (5) | (4) | (3) | (2) | (1) |
| 13 | | | | | | | |
| 14 | | | | | | | |
| 15 | | | | | | | |
| 16 | | | | | | | |
| 17 | | | | | | | |
| 18 | (7) | (6) | (5) | (4) | (3) | (2) | (1) |
| 19 | | | | | | | |
| 20 | (7) | (6) | (5) | (4) | (3) | (2) | (1) |
| 21 | | | | | | | |
| 22 | | | | | | | |
| 23 | | | | | | | |
| 24 | (7) | (6) | (5) | (4) | (3) | (2) | (1) |
| 25 | | | | | | | |
| 26 | | | | | | | |
| 27 | | | | | | | |
| 28 | (7) | (6) | (5) | (4) | (3) | (2) | (1) |
| 29 | (7) | (6) | (5) | (4) | (3) | (2) | (1) |
| 30 | (7) | (6) | (5) | (4) | (3) | (2) | (1) |
| 31 | | | | | | | |
| 32 | | | | | | | |
| 33 | | | | | | | |
| 34 | (7) | (6) | (5) | (4) | (3) | (2) | (1) |
| 35 | | | | | | | |
| 36 | (7) | (6) | (5) | (4) | (3) | (2) | (1) |

Add up all the Shaded Numbers to calculate your **Anxiety Score**.
Next, take that total and divide it by eighteen (18).

This is your score for attachment-related anxiety. It can range from 1 through 7. The higher the number, the more anxious you are about relationships.

Now add up all the Unshaded Numbers to calculate your **Avoidant Score**.
Next, take that total and divide it by eighteen (18).

This score indicates your attachment related avoidance. The higher the score, the more you avoid intimacy in relationships.

    1.5 - 2.5 = very low

    2.5 - 3.5 = low

    3.5 -4.5 = average

    4.5 -5.5 = high

    5.5 -6.5 = very high

Again, many of us score in both ranges, swinging from one level of connection to the other over time. The key is that in both cases, we do not trust the attachment to be secure.

Appendix  B

# *Male Gender Role Conformity Scale*

Please complete the questionnaire by circling the number which indicates your level of agreement or disagreement with each statement. Give only one answer for each statement.

| Strongly Disagree 1 | Disagree 2 | Slightly Disagree 3 | No Opinion 4 | Slightly Agree 5 | Agree 6 | Strongly Agree 7 |
|---|---|---|---|---|---|---|

|  | 1 | 2 | 3 | 4 | 5 | 6 | 7 |
|---|---|---|---|---|---|---|---|
| 1. I think homosexuals should never legally marry. |  |  |  |  |  |  |  |
| 2. I would only vote for a male President of the United States. |  |  |  |  |  |  |  |
| 3. I think men should be the leader in any group. |  |  |  |  |  |  |  |
| 4. I should be able to perform my job even if I am physically ill or hurt. |  |  |  |  |  |  |  |
| 5. I would never talk with a lisp because this is a sign of being gay. |  |  |  |  |  |  |  |
| 6. I would never wear make-up. |  |  |  |  |  |  |  |
| 7. I would rather watch football games instead of soap operas. |  |  |  |  |  |  |  |
| 8. I would vote to close down all homosexual bars. |  |  |  |  |  |  |  |
| 9. I am never interested in talk shows such as Oprah. |  |  |  |  |  |  |  |

| | 1 | 2 | 3 | 4 | 5 | 6 | 7 |
|---|---|---|---|---|---|---|---|
| 10. I believe men should excel at contact sports. | | | | | | | |
| 11. I would only give a boy an action figures not a doll. | | | | | | | |
| 12. I would never borrow money from friends or family members. | | | | | | | |
| 13. I believe men should have home improvement skills. | | | | | | | |
| 14. I should be able to fix most things around the house. | | | | | | | |
| 15. I would rather watch an action movie than a romantic film. | | | | | | | |
| 16. I think men always like to have sex. | | | | | | | |
| 17. I think homosexuals should not be allowed to serve in the military. | | | | | | | |
| 18. I would never compliment or flirt with another male. | | | | | | | |
| 19. I preferred to play with trucks rather than dolls. | | | | | | | |
| 20. I would never not turn down sex. Neither would most men. | | | | | | | |
| 21. I think a man should always be the boss. | | | | | | | |
| 22. I believe the man should provide the discipline in the family. | | | | | | | |
| 23. I would never hold hands or show affection toward another man. | | | | | | | |

| | 1 | 2 | 3 | 4 | 5 | 6 | 7 |
|---|---|---|---|---|---|---|---|
| 24. I think it is ok for me to use any and all means to "convince" a woman to have sex with me. | | | | | | | |
| 25. Gay men should never kiss another man in public. | | | | | | | |
| 26. I would never hold my wife's purse in public. | | | | | | | |
| 27. I believe I have to make my own way in the world. | | | | | | | |
| 28. I think I should always take the initiative when it comes to sex. | | | | | | | |
| 29. I never count on someone else to get the job done. | | | | | | | |
| 30. I think boys should not throw baseballs like girls. | | | | | | | |
| 31. I don't react when other people cry. | | | | | | | |
| 32. I would not continue a friendship with another man if I find out that the other man is gay. | | | | | | | |
| 33. When I am a little down in the dumps I don't think it is a good reason for me to act depressed. | | | | | | | |
| 34. If another man flirts with my wife when she is with me, this is a serious provocation and I should respond with aggression. | | | | | | | |
| 35. I think boys should be encouraged to find a means of demonstrating physical strengths. | | | | | | | |

| | 1 | 2 | 3 | 4 | 5 | 6 | 7 |
|---|---|---|---|---|---|---|---|
| 36. I should know how to repair my car if it breaks down. | | | | | | | |
| 37. I would bar gays from the teaching profession. | | | | | | | |
| 38. I never admit when others hurt my feelings. | | | | | | | |
| 39. I always get up to investigate if there is a strange noise in the house at night. | | | | | | | |
| 40. I don't bother with sex unless I can achieve an orgasm. | | | | | | | |
| 41. I think I should be detached in emotionally charged situations. | | | | | | | |
| 42. It is important for me to take risks, even if I might get hurt. | | | | | | | |
| 43. I am always be ready for sex. | | | | | | | |
| 44. I always want to be the major provider in my family. | | | | | | | |
| 45. When the going gets tough, I hunker down and get tougher. | | | | | | | |
| 46. I might find it a little silly or embarrassing if a male friend of mine cried over a sad love story. | | | | | | | |
| 47. It is my job as a father to teach my sons to mask fear. | | | | | | | |
| 48. I advise young men to be physically tough, even if he's not big. | | | | | | | |
| 49. In a group, it is a man's job to get things organized and moving ahead. | | | | | | | |

| | 1 | 2 | 3 | 4 | 5 | 6 | 7 |
|---|---|---|---|---|---|---|---|
| 50. People should not be able to tell how I am feeling by looking at my face. | | | | | | | |
| 51. I believe the man should make the final decisions involving money. | | | | | | | |
| 52. I am disappointed when I learn that a famous athlete is gay. | | | | | | | |
| 53. I am not too quick to tell others that I care about them. | | | | | | | |

**Scoring subscales and total score**

To obtain subscale scores compute the means of the items for that scale. These are designated below by the number as they appear on the score sheet.

Avoidance of Femininity = (6+7+9+11+15+19+26+30) /8

Homophobia = (1+5+8+17+18+23+25+32+37+52) /10

Extreme Self-Reliance = (4+12+13+14+27+29+36) /7

Focus on Toughness or Aggression = (10+34+35+39+42+45+48) /7

Achievement/Status) = (2+3+21+22+44+49+51) /7

Non-relational Attitudes and Objectify Sexuality = (16+20+24+28+40+43) /6

Restricted Emotions = (31+33+38+41+46+47+50+53) /8

The range for each subscale score is from 1-7, with higher scores indicating higher levels of endorsement of traditional masculinity role and lower scores indicating gender role conflict.

   1.5 - 2.5 =  high gender role conflict

   2.5 - 3.5 =  gender role conflict

   3.5 -4.5 =  average gender role conformity

   4.5 -5.5 =  high gender role conformity

   5.5 -6.5 =  very high gender role conformity

To obtain Total Score, take the mean of all of the items =  Your total of all scales/53

## Appendix C

# *Attachment Implications in the Development of Chronic Stress Disorders*

Maunder and Hunter[1] searched the literature on attachment insecurity over the last 35 years. They found that attachment insecurity contributes to physical illness, and determined three mechanisms through which attachment insecurity leads to disease risk: increased susceptibility to stress, increased use of external regulators of affect and altered help-seeking behavior. "The attachment model explains how repeated crucial interactions between infant and caregiver result in lifelong patterns of stress-response, receptivity to social support, and vulnerability to illness."

According to a new study published by the American Psychological Association, people who feel insecure about their attachments to others might be at higher risk for cardiovascular problems than those who feel secure in their relationships. "This is the first study to examine adult attachment and a range of specific health conditions," said lead author Lachlan A. McWilliams, PhD, of Acadia University.[2] He and a colleague examined data on 5,645 adults age 18 to 60 from the National Cormorbidity Survey Replication and found that people who felt insecure in relationships or avoided getting close to others might be at a higher risk of developing several chronic diseases. They found ratings of attachment insecurity were positively associated with a wide range of health problems, "Much of the health research regarding attachment has focused on pain conditions, so we were initially surprised that some of our strongest findings involved conditions related to the cardiovascular system," said McWilliams.

Participants rated themselves on three attachment styles: secure, avoidant and anxious. Secure attachment refers to feeling able to get close to others and being willing to have others depend on you. Avoidant attachment refers to difficulty getting close to and trusting others. Anxious attachment refers to the tendency to worry about rejection, feel needy and suspect others are reluctant to get close to you.

The participants filled out a medical history questionnaire which focused on arthritis, chronic back or neck problems, frequent or severe headaches, other forms of chronic pain, seasonal allergies, stroke and heart attack. They also disclosed whether a doctor had told them they had heart disease, high blood pressure, asthma, chronic lung disease, diabetes or high blood sugar, ulcers, epilepsy, seizures or cancer. They were also questioned regarding their history of psychological disorders.

After adjusting for demographic variables that could account for the health conditions, the authors found that avoidant attachment was positively associated with conditions defined primarily by pain (e.g. frequent or severe headaches). Anxious attachment was positively associated with a wider range of health conditions, including some defined primarily by pain and several involving the cardiovascular system (e.g. stroke, heart attack or high blood pressure).

The authors also adjusted for lifetime histories of common psychological disorders and found that people with anxious attachments were at a higher risk of chronic pain, stroke, heart attack, high blood pressure and ulcers. "These findings suggest that insecure attachment may be a risk factor for a wide range of health problems, particularly cardiovascular diseases. Longitudinal research on this topic is needed to determine whether insecure attachment predicts the development of cardiovascular disease and the occurrence of cardiovascular events, such as heart attacks," said McWilliams. "The findings also raise the possibility that interventions aimed at improving attachment security could also have positive health outcomes."

Attachment insecurity contributes to physical illness through increased susceptibility to stress. For example, anxious, preoccupied attachment involves a self-perception of vulnerability, which may lead to a lower threshold for activating attachment behavior. In this model of hypochondriasis and somatization, anxiously attached people preoccupied with attachment loss have developed a sense of personal vulnerability and vigilance so intense that normal perception of physiological operations is perceived as a potential threat.[3] This means bodily responses and sensations could be interpreted as a sign of increasing distress or a "problem." Another example is that avoidant attachment involves an attitude of heightened interpersonal distrust, such that situations requiring intimacy or interdependence (including a situation of apparent "social support") may be perceived as threatening.

Attachment insecurity contributes to physical illness through increasing the intensity or duration of the physiological stress response. For example, Sroufe and Waters[4] measured changes in heart rate in children during the Strange Situation. Heart rate acceleration reflects an aversive or defensive response, and heart rate deceleration reflects attention to the stimulus. The study reported that all children show heart-rate increases during separation, which remain elevated until reunion with the parent. At reunion, secure infants exhibit a soothing calm, returning to their baseline heart rate in less than a minute. Both ambivalent and avoidant children exhibit elevations of heart rate much longer into the reunion sequence, experiencing greater stress. Ambivalent infants request to be put down before their heart rates recovered to the pre-separation level. Then after being put down, with their heart rates still elevated, they reach up to be held again. Avoidant children show an increased heart rate from the beginning of separation until long into the reunion, despite the fact that they display very little distress. These stress response patterns become habitual and eventually account for susceptibility to physical illness.

Attachment insecurity contributes to physical illness through decreased stress buffering through social support. Secure individuals perceive more available support, and seek out that support more at times of stress than avoidant or ambivalent (preoccupied) individuals.[5,6,7] Social support is widely considered to be beneficial to a range of health outcomes. Perceiving support as threatening or nonexistent, then, endangers one's health.

Attachment insecurity contributes to physical illness through increased use of external regulators of affect. Since insecure attachment results in deficits in internal affect regulation,[8,9] insecurity is associated with greater use of external regulators. A number of behavioral strategies that are used to regulate dysphoric affect (to soothe, to distract or to excite) are also risk factors for disease, including smoking tobacco, drinking alcohol, using other psychoactive drugs, over-eating, under-eating and engaging in risky sexual activity. For example, adults with avoidant attachment tend to drink alcohol to enhance positive affect. External regulation of negative emotions through food intake has been shown to be a mechanism responsible for obesity.[10] Also, attachment style has a strong influence on sexual behavior.[11] So any tendency to use substances or external behaviors to reduce stress constitute an increased risk for physical illness.

Finally, attachment insecurity contributes to physical illness through the failure or nonuse of protective factors, such as social support, treatment adherence and symptom reporting. In the absence of positive body image, sensitivity to bodily needs and sense of self-control that develop along with secure attachment, health crises may produce defensiveness, especially denial. Denial of physical condition and needs during a health crisis results in an inability to benefit from supportive resources, and increases risk. Two studies directly support the link between attachment insecurity and symptom reporting. Avoidant attachment individuals tend to report symptoms less often, relying on emotional self-control instead.[12] Anxious and preoccupied individuals tend to report an excess of medically unexplained symptoms compared with securely attached individuals with the same disease.[13,14]

Abuse or neglect in childhood contributes to increased risk in adulthood for terminal disease. Felitti et al.[15] found a strong graded relationship between the breadth of exposure to abuse or household dysfunction during childhood and multiple risk factors for several of the leading causes of death in adults. Seven categories of adverse childhood experiences were studied: psychological, physical or sexual abuse; violence against mother; or living with household members who were substance abusers, mentally ill or suicidal, or ever imprisoned. The health risk factors were: heart disease, cancer, chronic lung disease, skeletal fractures, and liver disease. Persons who had experienced four or more categories of childhood exposure, compared to those who had experienced none, had four-fold to twelve-fold increased health risks for alcoholism, drug abuse, depression, and suicide attempts.

1. Maunder, R. G., & Hunter, J. J. (2001). Attachment and psychosomatic medicine: Developmental contributions to stress and disease. Psychosomatic Medicine, 63(4), 556-567. p. 556.

2. Lachlan A. McWilliams, PhD, and S. Jeffrey Bailey, PhD "Associations Between Adult Attachment Ratings and Health Conditions: Evidence From the National Comorbidity Survey Replication," Acadia University; *Health Psychology*, Vol. 29.

3. Stuart, S., & Noyes, R. (1999). Attachment and interpersonal communication in somatization. Psychosomatics, 40, 34-43.

4. Sroufe, L. A., & Waters, E. (1977). Heart rate as a convergent measure in clinical and developmental research. Merrill-Palmer Quarterly, 23, 3-27.

5. Florian, V., & Mikulincer, M. (1995). Effects of adult attachment style on the perception and search for social support. Journal of Psychology, 129, 665-676.

6. Mikulincer, M., & Florian, V. (1995). Appraisal of and coping with a real-life stressful situation: The contribution of attachment styles. Personality and Social Psychology Bulletin, 21, 406-414.

7. Ognibene, T. C., & Collins, N. L. (1998). Adult attachment styles, perceived social support, and coping strategies. Journal of Social and Personal Relationships, 15, 323-345.

8. Simpson, J. A., Rholes, W. S., & Nelligan, J. S. (1992). Support seeking and support giving within couples in an anxiety-provoking situation: The role of attachment styles. Journal of Personality & Social Psychology, 62, 434-446.

9. House, J. S., Landis, K. R., & Umberson, D. (1988). Social relationships and health. Science, 241, 540-545.

10. Kobak, R., & Sceery, A. (1988). Attachment in late adolescence: Working models, affect regulation, and representation of self and others. Child Development, 59, 135-146.

11. Mikulincer, M. (1999). Adult attachment style and affect regulation: Strategic variation in self-appraisals. Journal of Personality and Social Psychology, 75, 420-435.

12. Magai, C. (1999). Affect, imagery and attachment. In J. Cassidy & P. R. Shaver (Eds.), Handbook of Attachment: Theory, Research and Clinical Applications, 787-802. New York: Guilford Press.

13. Raynes, E., Auerbach, C., & Botyanski, N. C. (1989). Level of object representation and psychic structure deficit in obese persons. Psychological Reports, 64, 291-294.

14. Feeney, J. A., & Raphael, B. (1992). Adult attachments and sexuality: Implications for understanding risk behaviours for HIV infection. Australia and New Zealand Journal of Psychiatry, 26, 399-407.

15. Felitti VJ, Anda RF, Nordenberg D et al: The relationship of **adult health** status to **childhood abuse** & household dysfunction. *American Journal of Preventive Medicine* 14(4):245-258, May 1998

Appendix D

## *Adrenal Fatigue Questionnaire*

# Dr. Wilson's Adrenal Fatigue Questionnaire

**From Adrenal Fatigue: The 21st Century Stress Syndrome**
**by Dr. James L. Wilson**

This questionnaire covers many of the common fatigue causes and stress symptoms associated with fatigued adrenals. Although not meant to be a stand-alone diagnostic tool, this stress quiz can be helpful in indicating the presence and degree of adrenal fatigue.

Instructions: Please enter the appropriate response number to each statement in the columns below. Use the values in the rating scale below. Once you have answered all of the questions total them up following the instructions below.

Note: One column in the questionnaire is titled "Past" and another "Now." The past refers to the last time you felt well. If you cannot determine a specific date, then pick a relative time after which your symptoms seemed to noticeably worsen. It is helpful to write this date down so you do not forget it. All your responses in the "Past" column will be about how you felt before that date. The "Now" column is not necessarily about today, but about how you generally feel now, in this present time frame or since the date you entered for the "Past" column.

**Rating Scale**

| 0 | Never/Rarely |
|---|---|
| 1 | Occasionally/Slightly |
| 2 | Moderate in Intensity and Frequency |
| 3 | Intense/Severe or Frequent |

| Past | Now | |
|------|-----|---|
| | | **Predisposing Factors** |
| | | I have experienced long periods of stress that have affected my well being. |
| | | I have had one or more severely stressful events that have affected my well being. |
| | | I have driven myself to exhaustion. |
| | | I overwork with little play or relaxation for extended periods. |
| | | I have had extended, severe or recurring respiratory infections. |
| | | I have taken long term or intense steroid therapy (corticosteroids). |
| | | I tend to gain weight, especially around the middle (spare tire). |
| | | I have a history of alcoholism and/or drug abuse. |
| | | I have environmental sensitivities. |
| | | I have diabetes (Type II, adult onset, NIDDM). |
| | | I suffer from post-traumatic stress syndrome. |
| | | * I suffer from anorexia. |
| | | I have one or more other chronic illnesses or diseases. |
| | | |
| | | **Key Signs and Symptoms** |
| | | My ability to handle stress or pressure has decreased. |
| | | I am less productive at work. |
| | | I seem to have decreased in cognitive ability. I don't think as clearly as I used to. |
| | | My thinking is confused when hurried or under pressure. |
| | | I tend to avoid emotional situations. |
| | | I tend to shake or am nervous when under pressure. |
| | | I suffer from nervous stomach indigestion when tense. |
| | | I have many unexplained fears/anxieties. |
| | | My sex drive is noticeably less than it used to be. |
| | | I get light-headed or dizzy when rising rapidly from a sitting or lying position. |

| Past | Now | |
|------|-----|---|
| | | I have feelings of graying or blacking out. |
| | | * I am chronically fatigued; a tiredness that is not usually relieved by sleep. |
| | | I feel unwell much of the time. |
| | | I notice that my ankles are swollen -- the swelling is worse in the evening. |
| | | I usually need to lie down or rest after sessions of psychological or emotional pressure/stress. |
| | | My muscles sometimes feel weaker than they should. |
| | | My hands and legs get restless -- experience meaningless body movements. |
| | | I have become allergic or have increased frequency/ severity of allergic reactions. |
| | | When I scratch my skin a white line remains for a minute or more. |
| | | Small, irregular dark brown spots have appeared on my forehead, face, neck and shoulders. |
| | | * I sometimes feel weak all over. |
| | | I have unexplained and frequent headaches. |
| | | I am frequently cold. |
| | | * I have a decreased tolerance for cold. |
| | | * I have low blood pressure. |
| | | I often become hungry, confused, shaky or somewhat paralyzed under stress. |
| | | I have lost weight without reason while feeling very tired and listless. |
| | | I have feelings of hopelessness and despair. |
| | | I have decreased tolerance. People irritate me more. |
| | | The lymph nodes in my neck are frequently swollen (I get swollen glands on my neck). |
| | | * I have times of nausea and vomiting for no apparent reason. |
| | | |

| Past | Now | |
|------|-----|---|
| | | **Energy Patterns** |
| | | I often have to force myself in order to keep going. Everything seems like a chore. |
| | | I am easily fatigued. |
| | | I have difficulty getting up in the morning (don't really wake up until about 10:00 AM). |
| | | I suddenly run out of energy. |
| | | I usually feel much better and fully awake after the noon meal. |
| | | I often have an afternoon low between 3:00-5:00 PM. |
| | | I get low on energy, moody or foggy if I do not eat regularly. |
| | | I usually feel my best after 6:00 PM. |
| | | I am often tired at 9:00-10:00 pm, but resist going to bed. |
| | | I like to sleep late in the morning. |
| | | My best, most refreshing sleep often comes between 7:00-9:00 AM. |
| | | I often do my best work late at night (early in the morning). |
| | | If I don't go to bed by 11:00 PM, I get a second burst of energy around 11:00 PM, often lasting until 1:00-2:00 AM. |
| | | |
| | | **Frequently Observed Events** |
| | | I get coughs/colds that stay around for several weeks. |
| | | I have frequent, recurring bronchitis, pneumonia or other respiratory infections. |
| | | I get asthma, colds, and other respiratory involvements two or more times per year. |
| | | I frequently get rashes, dermatitis, or other skin conditions. |
| | | I have rheumatoid arthritis. |
| | | I have allergies to several things in the environment. |
| | | I have multiple chemical sensitivities. |
| | | I have chronic fatigue syndrome. |

| Past | Now | |
|------|-----|---|
| | | I get pain in the muscles of my upper back and lower neck for no apparent reason. |
| | | I get pain in the muscles in the side of my neck. |
| | | I have insomnia or difficulty sleeping. |
| | | I have fibromyalgia. |
| | | I suffer from asthma. |
| | | I suffer from hay fever. |
| | | I suffer from nervous breakdowns. |
| | | My allergies are becoming worse (more severe, frequent or diverse). |
| | | The fat pads on palms of my hands and/or tips of my fingers are often red. |
| | | I bruise more easily than I used to. |
| | | I have tenderness in my back near my spine at the bottom of my ribcage when pressed. |
| | | I have swelling under my eyes upon rising that goes away after I have been up for a couple of hours. |
| | | (Women Only) I have increasing symptoms of premenstrual syndrome (PMS) such as cramps, bloating, moodiness, irritability, emotional instability, headaches, tiredness, and/or intolerance before my period (only some of these need be present). |
| | | (Women Only) My periods are generally heavy but they often stop, or almost stop, on the fourth day, only to start up profusely on the 5th or 6th day. |
| | | |
| | | **Food Patterns** |
| | | I need coffee or some other stimulant to get going in the morning. |
| | | I often crave food high in fat and feel better with high fat foods. |
| | | I use high fat foods to drive myself. |
| | | I often use high fat foods and caffeine containing drinks (coffee, colas, chocolate) to drive myself. |

| Past | Now | |
|------|-----|---|
| | | I often crave salt and/or foods high in salt. I like salty foods. |
| | | I feel worse if I eat high potassium foods (like bananas, figs, raw potatoes), especially if I eat them in the morning. |
| | | I crave high protein foods (meats, cheeses). |
| | | I crave sweet foods (pies, cakes, pastries, doughnuts, dried fruits, candies or desserts.) |
| | | I feel worse if I miss or skip a meal. |
| | | |
| | | **Aggravating Patterns** |
| | | I have constant stress in my life or work. |
| | | My dietary habits tend to be sporadic and unplanned. |
| | | My relationships at work and/or home are unhappy. |
| | | I do not exercise regularly. |
| | | I eat lots of fruit. |
| | | My life contains insufficient enjoyable activities. |
| | | I have little control over how I spend my time. |
| | | I restrict my salt intake. |
| | | I have gum and/or tooth infections or abscesses. |
| | | I have meals at irregular times. |
| | | |
| | | **Relieving Factors** |
| | | I feel better almost right away once a stressful situation is resolved. |
| | | Regular meals decrease the severity of my symptoms. |
| | | I often feel better after spending a night out with friends. |
| | | I often feel better if I lie down. |

**Interpreting your Adrenal Fatigue Questionnaire**

**Total Count of Questions Answered:**

| Past | |
|------|--|
| Now | |

This gives you a general "Yes or No" answer to the question, "Do I have adrenal fatigue?" Look at your "Total number of questions answered" above. The purpose of this score is to see the total number of signs and symptoms of adrenal fatigue you have. There are a total of 87 questions for men and 89 questions for women in the questionnaire. If you responded to more than **26** (men) or **32** (women) of the questions, regardless of which severity response number you gave the question, you have some degree of adrenal fatigue. The greater the number of questions that you responded to, the greater your adrenal fatigue. If you responded affirmatively to less than 20 of the questions, it is unlikely that adrenal fatigue is your problem. People who do not have adrenal fatigue may still experience a few of these indicators in their lives, but not many of them. If your symptoms do not include fatigue or decreased ability to handle stress, then you are probably not suffering from adrenal fatigue.

**Total Points:**

| Past | |
|------|--|
| Now | |

The total points are used to determine the degree of severity of your ad-renal fatigue. If you ranked every question 3 (the worst) your total points would be 261 for men and 267 for women. If you scored under **40**, you either have only slight adrenal fatigue or none at all. If you scored between **44-87** for men or **45-88** for women, then overall you have a mild degree of adrenal fatigue. This does not mean that some individual symptoms are not severe, but overall your symptom picture reflects mildly fatigued ad-renals. If you scored between **88-130** for men or **89-132** for women, your adrenal fatigue is moderate. If you scored above **130** for men or **132** for women, the consider yourself to be suffering from severe adrenal fatigue. Now compare the total points of the different sections with each other. This allows you to see if 1 or 2 of the sections stand out as having more signs and symptoms. They will be the most useful ones for you to watch as indicators as you improve. Seeing which sections stand out will also be helpful in developing your own recovery program.

**Severity Index:**

| Past | |
|------|--|
| Now | |

The severity index is calculated by simply dividing the total points by the total number of questions you answered in the affirmative. It gives an indication of how severely you experience the signs and symptoms, with **1.0-1.6** being mild, **1.7-2.3** being moderate, and **2.4-3.0** being severe. This number is especially useful for those who suffer from only a few of these signs and symptoms, but yet are considerably debilitated by them.

**Interpretation of the "Predisposing Factors" Section:**

| Past | |
|------|--|
| Now | |

This section helps determine which factors led to the development of your adrenal fatigue. There may have been only one factor or there may have been several, but the number does not matter. One severely stressful incident can be all it takes for someone to develop adrenal fatigue, although typically it is more. This list is not exhaustive, but the items listed in this section are the most common factors that lead to adrenal fatigue. Use this section to better understand how your adrenal fatigue developed. Seeing how it started often makes clearer what actions you can take to successfully recover from it.

**Key Factor Score:**

| Now | |
|-----|--|

This is the sum of the answers to the questions marked by an asterisk (*) for the "Now" column. If this total is more than **9**, we strongly recommend that you consult a physician who is familiar with stress and adrenal function.

**The Author**

If you wish to contact Mary please feel free to call, send an email, or a letter.

Mary Crocker Cook

1710 Hamilton Ave. #8

San Jose, CA 95125.

Phone: (408) 448-0333

Email: marycook@connectionscounselingassociates.com

For more information about Mary's counseling services or presentation topics visit:

www.marycrockercook.com

**The Editor**

Howard Scott Warshaw received his Masters of Arts from JFK University and Masters of Engineering from Tulane University. After decades as a software designer/programmer, award winning filmaker, celebrated video game developer, author, teacher, and engineering manager. Howard integrates his eclectic skill set in the service of others as a psychotherapist. He is currently in practice in Los Altos where he focuses on the unique needs of Silicon Valley's Hi-Tech community. Howard can be found at: www.hswarshaw.com

Lightning Source UK Ltd.
Milton Keynes UK
UKOW02f0302100915

258370UK00001B/136/P